PRAYING
WITH
WOMEN OF
THE BIBLE

PRAYING
WITH
WOMEN OF
THE BIBLE

Bridget Mary Meehan

LIGUORI/TRIUMPH
LIGUORI, MISSOURI

Published by Liguori/Triumph
An imprint of Liguori Publications
Liguori, Missouri
www.liguori.org

Library of Congress Cataloging-in-Publication Data

Meehan, Bridget Mary.
    Praying with women of the Bible / Bridget Mary Meehan. — 1st ed.
        p. cm.
    ISBN 0-7648-0231-3 (pkb.)
    1. Women in the Bible—Meditations. 2. Women—Prayer-books and
devotions—English. I. Title.
BS575.M47   1998
242'.643—dc21   98–3176

Unless otherwise indicated, scriptural citations are from the *New Revised
Standard Version*, copyright 1989, Division of Christian Education of the
National Council of Churches of Christ in the United States of America. All
rights reserved. Used with permission.

Printed in the United States of America
08 07 06 05 04   7 6 5 4 3

DEDICATION

To my family:
my parents Bridie and Jack, my Aunt Molly McCarthy,
my brothers Sean and Patrick, my sisters-in-law Nancy
and Valerie, my niece and nephew Katie and Danny.

To all the women whose courage, strength, and wisdom have re-
flected to me the love of God as Sister and Friend? especially Regina
Madonna Oliver, Irene Marshall, Sandra Voelker, Phyllis Hurst,
Mary Beben, Rea Howarth, Ann Tennison, Eileen Thomas, Pat
Zimmerman, Sharon and Kerry Danner, Peggy Gott, Joni Whelan,
Marcia Tibbitts, Betty Wade, Susan Curcio, Patricia Byrne, Patricia
McAleavy, Kathleen Bulger, Eileen Dohn, Peg Bowen, Estelle
Spachman, Elizabeth Cerrato, Ginger Avvenire, Ginny Koenig,
Rosemary Walsh, Debbie Dubuque, Mary Fitzgibbons, Megan Fitz-
gibbons, Patricia Herlihy, Mary Guertin, Mary Kay Salomone,
Kathleen Wiesberg, Donna Mogan, Nancy Healy, Maureen Miela,
Consilia Karli, Kay Graf, Olga Gane, Evelyn Mulhall, Mary Patricia
Mulhall, Kathleen Mulhall, Eileen Kelly, Eugenia Garrido, Mary
Ambrosia, Gavita King, Dawn Vehmeier, Mary Jean Kane, Ellen
Coakley, Helen Groff, Luz Sandiego, Roseanne Fedorko, Lynn
Johnson, Daisy Sullivan, Michal Morches, Rochelle Applewhite,
Maria Billick, Doris Mason, Cathy Kopac, Lisa Jarvis, Vera Cole,
Kaye Brown, Mary Anna Kelley, Rita Satriano, and the Sisters for
Christian Community.

To all the Celtic women in my family:
Noreen Davy, Molly Meehan, Mary D. Meehan, Mary Ferns, Peg
Meehan, Margaret Ryan, Mary Tregent, Esther Meehan, Tess
Murphy, Elizabeth Murphy, Catherine Murphy, Rose Meehan,

Katherine Meehan, Marion Meehan, Kathleen McNamara, Mary Meehan, Alice Meehan, Eileen Meehan, and Eileen Preston.

To Mary, mother and disciple of Jesus, whose companionship reflects sisterly love in the power of Sophia-God.

To all our foremothers and foresisters in the faith: Companions, Champions, and Change-Agents.

To all women who live and love as courageous disciples of Jesus in the contemporary world.

CONTENTS

᷾

INTRODUCTION

W omen today want to hear about other women's struggles to live spiritual lives. They search for female counterparts in the scriptures and in the tradition. In this time of biblical renaissance, women long to hear the Good News through the words and lives of women in the Bible. They desire to make connections between their own lives and those of strong female role models: women who were prophets, visionaries, activists, saints, martyrs, and heroines.

Praying With Women of the Bible came into being from my own encounters with valiant women in the Bible. As I began to reflect prayerfully on the memorable women in the Book of Books, I discovered that the ancient stories have powerful messages for women today. Each of these remarkable women is a sister, a friend, and a mentor who shares her gifts, experiences, relationships, and accomplishments with us. In each one's life we contemplate a living feminine person whose life exemplifies daring or creativity or insight or shrewdness or compassion or faithfulness, or combinations of these and other virtues, in the face of hostility, indifference, and discrimination.

In the Hebrew scriptures we meet strong matriarchs Sarah and Hagar. Laughing Sarah lifts our spirits as she waits patiently for God to fulfill the divine promises. Hagar, who suffers exploitation in the house of Sarah and Abraham, is vindicated by God and becomes the only person in the Bible to name God. Daring sisters such as Miriam, Deborah, Ruth, Esther, and Judith, took initiative, collaborated with others in difficult situations, challenged oppression, and affirmed life. Women who study the Bible today can identify and make connections with these convincing, intelligent, activist women.

The women of the Christian scriptures such as Mary, the mother of Jesus, the woman with the flow of blood, the Canaanite woman, the Samaritan woman, Martha, Mary of Magdala, and the woman who anoints Jesus' head offer hope-filled stories of the Jesus who can liberate, heal, and empower women as well as men today. As disciples and equals with the male followers of Christ, these women of the gospel were chosen by Christ to proclaim the Good News of the inclusivity of God's reign: that all people are welcome at the banquet table, especially the downtrodden, marginalized, rejected, and powerless.

In the early Church, we encounter the teaching, preaching, and leadership of women such as Junia, Phoebe, Priscilla, Lydia, and Mary, the mother of John Mark—all confident, independent, generous, faithful women, aware of their spiritual power and authority. The story of Thecla, a woman apostle who appears in the apocryphal book *Acts of Paul and Thecla*, reveals the tremendous impact of women's solidarity in times of opposition, crisis, and rejection.

The convincing women whose powerful testimony and activist lives fill the pages of this book are radiant reflections of the feminine face of God. They show us how to be strong witnesses to the Holy One in our midst. These women invite us to experience woman-courage, woman-hope, woman-strength, woman-wisdom, and woman-passion. Their spirit liberates, energizes, and empowers us. Dialogue with these models of faith. Establish a relationship with these companions, champions, and change-agents among us. Argue with these prophetic witnesses to the gospel! Question their decisions! Listen to their insights! Share your own story with them! They are our sisters and friends. Their stories are our stories. Their words are a source of inspiration and an incentive to renewal in our commitment to work for justice, peace, and equality in our world. We can learn much about faith, hope, and love from these daring disciples.

From all over the world, sisters, daughters, mothers, grandmothers, women of many cultures, races, and ethnic backgrounds are sharing their dreams and visions to birth a new paradigm of worship, prayer, and community. As the bondage of sexism, racism, militarism, and ageism continues, women's prayer groups have sprung up in many places and are exploring a rich variety of resources that celebrate the stories and spirituality of women.

Praying With Women of the Bible invites you to catch the living spirit of amazing witnesses to the inbreaking of God's wondrous, passionate, infinite Love-with-us. In the reflections, discussion questions, prayer experiences, and guided meditations that follow, you are invited to reflect on each sister in the faith, to imaginatively recreate her story from your perspective, and to reflect on her words and actions in light of your experiences. This book invites you to experience a sense of solidarity with women, not unlike ourselves, who were mothers, daughters, wives, sisters, friends, servants, widows, prophets, leaders, seekers, ministers, martyrs, and apostles. As a resource for women and men to celebrate their biblical heritage, this book provides new hope for all who seek the Spirit's empowerment in their lives. It reaffirms for today's woman that nothing is impossible with God. Like our biblical sisters, who took initiative, contemporary women can dream new dreams of liberation, healing, and empowerment for our world. We can act as if our vision for equality, justice, and love is already happening, because it is! The inbreaking of God's love through the gifts and empowerment of women is already a reality!

Each of the prayer experiences begins with introductory material that provides a brief background on the life of one of these biblical women. After that you will find a reflection drawn from the actions or writings of the individual, four discussion questions, and seven suggestions for prayer to help you contemplate the depths of divine love that this particular woman-model reveals for your spiritual journey.

In the prayer experiences, I recommend that you use a variety of approaches. Some possibilities are journaling, poetry, dance, body movement, mime, drama, song, or some artistic response like drawing, painting, sculpting, playing with clay, stamping, or needlepoint. You may wish to use some of the prayer suggestions provided in each prayer experience as a guided meditation; or you may choose to skip around, trying a different one each time you reflect on a biblical woman's life. Listen to your subconscious and try what attracts or excites you. Be conscious of what nourishes your creative spirit and do that!

Groups could use one or more of the discussion questions to get people talking about the contributions of these women and their impact on our hearts and lives. Background music—specifically classical or instrumental—may provide an appropriate setting for reflection and sharing. Before beginning, the group should decide on a facilitator to lead the guided prayer for them, and organize materials and space for art, journaling, story, body movement, creative activity, and so forth. After everything is ready, the facilitator reads aloud one or more of the prayer experiences, and allows time for reflection and response. Groups could then share their experiences and/or their responses to the discussion starters. Larger groups could break into groups of five or six for the discussion.

Groups could also design creative rituals celebrating the

powerful women's stories that appear in this book. One simple way of doing this is for the group to select music for the prayer experience(s) and movements to accompany the music in which group members can participate. This ritual could begin and/or conclude each session. Singing, humming, dancing, clapping, tapping, moving, swaying to music, and joining hands with others involves us in body prayer that helps us to connect with each other in deep ways.

Another suggestion is that group members could decide ahead of time to bring to the next session a symbol of the biblical woman the group is contemplating. Then, at the conclusion of the prayer experience, the members of the group could take turns sharing the symbols they brought. After each member shares, she puts the symbol on a special table decorated with cloth, candles, and flowers. The group then prays a litany, or spontaneous prayers, sings a song, does a circle dance, and/or engages in a group hug. Different members could take turns preparing one of these prayer rituals for each session.

Another idea for communal prayer is that groups choose one or more of the following elements for worship: water, oil, incense, bread, wine, or an art object such as a drawing, painting, or sculpture. Then the group creates a simple ritual such as washing of hands, anointing each other with oil, passing the art object around in the group, or breaking and eating bread together to celebrate the impact the biblical woman has on people today. These simple rituals, which can be accompanied by formal or spontaneous prayer, are moving worship experiences that not only deepen the group members' relationships with heroic women, but also help the group members become a caring community.

Yet another suggestion is to use the senses—visual, auditory, tactile, and olfactory—in inclusive, communal prayer to open ourselves to the Spirit's movement among us. Groups can design rituals in which members look at beautiful art, listen to melodic music, smell perfumed incense, touch soft clay, and/or eat delicious food. This prayer approach invites the group to savor spiritual experiences in rich and often unexpected ways. Resource books that have a variety of ideas for communal rituals are *Women Prayer Services* by Iben Gjerding and Katherine Kinnamon (Twenty-Third Publications); *We Are the Circle* by Julie Howard (Liturgical Press) and the three-volume feminist lectionary series: *WomanWord*, *WomanWitness*, and *WomanWisdom* by Miriam Therese Winter (Crossroad).

The wind blows where it wills. Be open to the laughter, tears, insight, and wonder that the group may experience as it prays together. There are no right or wrong ways of doing communal prayer. Different things work for different groups. The important thing is to explore together, experiment together, share together, pray together, and celebrate together these daring women role models. With this book, I invite you to experience the rich legacy of spiritual empowerment that twenty dynamic, committed women of faith have shared. As you encounter these soul sisters, may you dance merrily together in God's liberating, loving presence!

PRAYING
WITH
WOMEN OF
THE BIBLE

SARAH

✍

S arah is the first matriarch of Israel. Her story is found in Genesis 12–23. According to the scripture, Sarah is a beautiful woman who marries Abraham . On two occasions Abraham identified Sarah as his sister for his own self-interests. On one of those occasions, when Abraham and Sarah were facing famine, they traveled to Egypt. Abraham came up with a plan for his survival that involved giving Sarah to the Egyptians. He said to Sarah, "I know well that you are a woman beautiful in appearance; and when the Egyptians see you they will say, 'This is his wife'; then they will kill me....Say you are my sister, so that it may go well with me because of you, and that my life may be spared on your account" (Gn 12:11–13).

The narrative then tells us that the Egyptians take Sarah into Pharaoh's house, and give Abraham the deal of his life: "sheep, oxen, male donkeys, male and female slaves, female donkeys, and camels" (12:16). Pharaoh falls for the deception and Abraham becomes rich. God saves Sarah by inflicting several plagues upon the pharaoh and his house. The result: Pharaoh realizes that he has committed adultery. He confronts Abraham: "What is this you have done to me?...Why did you say, 'She is my sister,' so that I took her for my wife? Now then, here is your wife, take her, and be gone" (12:18–19). Sarah's thoughts and feelings during this ordeal are not reported. Is she the victim of Abraham's desire to save himself at her expense? Or did she go along willingly with

Abraham's deception? The text provides no clues. Sarah is silent.

In chapter 11 and chapter 16, the narrator tells us that Sarah is barren. In the Hebrew culture, barrenness was one of the greatest afflictions that could befall anyone. Motherhood was extolled by the rabbis as the heart of women's identity because it preserved the ancestral line. Sarah was barren, according to the story, until she was ninety years old. Unable to conceive, Sarah gave Hagar, her Egyptian slave-girl, to Abraham as a surrogate mother: "You see that the Lord has prevented me from bearing children; go in to my slave-girl; it may be that I shall obtain children by her" (16:2). When Sarah gave Hagar to Abraham as a secondary wife, Hagar's status was enhanced. Sarah also thought that her status would increase by the birth of a child to this union. But after Hagar became pregnant, things did not work out as Sarah planned. Author Trevor Dennis notes: "Hagar has turned the tables on her. The utterly powerless foreign slave has shown what female power there is to be found in fertility, and what degradation lies in barrenness."[1] After Hagar slept with Abraham, she became pregnant and gave birth to Ishmael. Problems soon developed between Sarah and Hagar. Sarah complained bitterly to Abraham that Hagar looked at her with contempt after she conceived. Sarah blamed Abraham for her pain: "May the wrong done to me be on you!" (16:5). But Abraham, trying to get out of a tight spot, told Sarah to do what she wished with her maid. Then Sarah abused Hagar.

In Genesis 17, God tells Abraham that Sarah and he will bear a child. Abraham is incredulous and falls on his face laughing and saying: "Can a child be born to a man who is a hundred years old? Can Sarah who is ninety years old bear a child?" But God answers, "...your wife Sarah shall bear you a son, and you shall name him Isaac. I will establish my covenant with him as an everlasting covenant for his offspring after him. As for Ishmael,...I will bless him and...make him a great nation" (17:17–20). When Sarah overhears Abraham's conversation with the three angels who promise that she will give birth to a son, she laughs: "Sarah laughed to herself saying, 'After I have grown old, and my husband is old, shall I have pleasure?'" God, according to the narrative, takes offense and asks Abraham: "Why did Sarah laugh, and say, 'Shall I indeed bear a child now that I am old?'" Sarah denied her laughter, but God reproves her: "Oh yes, you did laugh" (18:13,15).

Why did God ignore Abraham's laughter and chastise Sarah for her chuckles? Some commentators point out that there is a double standard at work in the test. In the mind of the storyteller, Sarah does not take angelic messengers seriously, but Abraham is talking about the promise "man-to-man" with God. Therefore, his behavior is excused.

At a feast to celebrate Isaac's weaning, Sarah noticed Ishmael playing with her son. Immediately, she became incensed and ordered Abraham: "Cast out this slave woman with her son; for the son of this slave woman shall not inherit along with my son Isaac"(21:10). Finally, Sarah makes the decision to send Hagar and Ishmael away permanently. When Abraham complained to God, God replied to him "Do not be distressed...whatever Sarah says to you, do as she tells you..." (21:12). So Abraham prepared supplies, placed the child on Hagar's shoulders, and sent her into the wilderness.

Sharon Pace Jeansonne, associate professor of Hebrew Bible at Marquette University, thinks that

If there is any doubt as to whether Sarah's plan is justified, the narrator has God respond in a direct revelation to Abraham. Once again Abraham is reminded that his descendants will be given through Isaac. God confirms Sarah's plan; perhaps she understands God's will better than did Abraham all along.[2]

Commentator Savina J. Teubal does not agree. She does not think Sarah banished Ishmael because of a material inheritance but because she feared Ishmael would influence Isaac's religious training. For Sarah it was a cultural issue: She wanted Isaac brought up according to her religious beliefs and practices.[3]

Elsa Tamez points out that Sarah's appeal to Abraham to banish Ishmael violated the law of the time, which upheld the rights of an adopted child born of a slave. Therefore, in this case, Ishmael and Isaac shared equal rights to inheritance. Sarah used the law when it suited her and violated the law when it served her interests.[4]

Author Janice Nunnally-Cox believes the Bible portrays Sarah as an honored matriarch. She comments on the equal partnership that Sarah and Abraham shared:

He does not command her; she commands him, yet there seems to be an affectionate bond between them…The two have grown up together and grown old together, and when Sarah dies, Abraham can do nothing but weep.[5]

Other scholars disagree that Sarah and Abraham had an egalitarian marriage. Some think that Sarah was as much a victim as Hagar. According to this view, Sarah's story depicts patriarchy's focus on controlling women's sexuality. Sarah's role is limited by her being wife and mother. Author Miriam Therese Winter notes that "patriarchy condoned Abraham's passing his wife Sarah off as his sister because the molestation of her body was less an issue than his own physical safety."[6]

What can women learn from Sarah? One lesson is to treat other women—especially women from other cultures, races, religions—as sisters, companions, and equals. Women in contemporary society do not need to view other women as better or lesser than themselves. Women do not need be competitive, pitting their skills, knowledge, and accomplishments against other women in a win-lose manner. Women do not need to adopt a male patriarchal model that tries to dominate and subordinate other people for whatever reason. This is the way the world has worked up to now, and it continues to result in violence, destruction, and war in many parts of the globe. Instead, women can show humanity a new way to live in harmony and peace. We can begin this journey by affirming other women's gifts, recognizing our limitations, and celebrating our female bondedness with its infinite potential for love and empowerment. Second, women can learn from Sarah how to wait patiently for God to act in our lives. Sarah believed that the Faithful One would fufill the divine promises. Some things take a long time, and we need Sarah's perseverance. Third, Sarah reminds us to laugh at ourselves and at life's incongruities. It will lift our spirits especially during stressful times. Our laughing God, who created a world full of wonderful surprises for us, sometimes shows up in the funniest of places with a message guaranteed to knock our socks off with glee—as was the case with Sarah.

REFLECTION

"The angelic visitors said to Abraham, 'Where is your wife Sarah?' And Abraham said, 'There in the tent.' Then one said, 'I will surely return to you in due season, and your wife Sarah shall have a son.' And Sarah was listening at the tent entrance…. Now Sarah and Abraham were old, advanced in age; it had ceased to be with Sarah after the manner of women. So Sarah laughed to herself, saying, 'After I have grown old, and my husband is old shall I have pleasure?' The Lord said to Abraham 'Why did Sarah laugh, and say, "Shall I indeed bear a child, now that I am old?" Is anything too wonderful for the Lord? At the set time I will return to you, in due season, and Sarah shall have a son.' But Sarah denied saying, 'I did not laugh'; for she was afraid. God said, 'Oh yes, you did laugh'" (Gn 18:9–15).

"Sarah conceived and bore Abraham a son in his old age, at the time of which God had spoken to him. Abraham gave the name Isaac to his son whom Sarah bore him.... Now Sarah said, 'God has brought laughter for me; everyone who hears will laugh with me....Who would ever have said to Abraham that Sarah would nurse children? Yet I have borne him a son in his old age'" (Gn 21:2–3,6–7).

DISCUSSION STARTERS

1. Sarah is portrayed in the biblical text as a strong woman of faith. Do you know any strong women of faith in your life? If so, do they inspire you?

2. Sarah had a wonderful sense of humor. If you were Sarah, would you have laughed if you found out that you were about to become pregnant at ninety years old? Why is laughter good medicine for the soul? How can laughter help you deal with stress and grow spiritually?

3. In the Hebrew scriptures, a woman's value is often measured by her ability to bear children. What is the role of the matriarch? Reflect on the heritage you received from your mother, grandmothers, great-grandmothers, etc. What blessings have your received from the women in your family tradition?

4. How is Sarah a role model for contemporary women? If you could ask Sarah a question, what would it be?

PRAYER EXPERIENCE

1. Use some instrumental or classical music to relax. Or close your eyes and hum, chant, or sing a favorite lullaby. Let the music soothe you like a mother rocking her baby in her arms.
2. Be aware that God, the divine mother, holds you close and nurtures you with tenderness and love beyond all imagining.... Spend time in silence, simply embraced by love....
3. Listen as God speaks to you of wonderful blessings that are awaiting you...overpowering strength...overflowing grace...immense delight...transforming vision...radiant bliss...new life....
4. Remember your mother, grandmothers, great-grandmothers, the matriarchs of your ancestral line as far back as you can go.... Name each woman and invite her to join you around an imaginary circle to share your family story.... Invite each matriach to share with you a spiritual experience of faith, courage, prayer, joy, laughter, pain...whatever she chooses to pass on...to you, to your children, grandchildren, great-grandchildren, and so on.... Now invite Sarah, Hagar, Mary, or any spiritual matriach to share her story of woman-wisdom with you.... Before leaving this sacred space, dance together in a circle of love....
5. Reflect on Sarah's laughter...be aware of the amazing grace that flowed through her being as she felt God's love fill her emptiness with eager hope.... Listen to her peals of laughter echo through the ages giving women of all ages fresh delight in miracles that will never cease....

6. Smile for several minutes and be aware of any thoughts, feelings, insights, sensations that you experience…. Reflect on funny moments when you let go of inhibitions and burst into giggles or belly laughter. Experience the gift of laughter bubbling up from deep inside you…. Let it be your prayer of praise for the blessings and surprises of the God of Laughter in your life….

7. Create your own concluding prayer or use the following prayer:

> *Promise us,*
> *O God of Sarah,*
> *that you will be faithful forever*
> *especially in the times we experience*
> *discouragement and emptiness.*
> *O God of the Unexpected,*
> *teach us to laugh heartily at life's*
> *inconsistencies and at our own silly pretenses.*
> *Surprise us, as you did Sarah, with new life,*
> *fresh hope, and energetic love.*
> *Then, like Sarah, we will praise you with glad*
> *hearts and grateful laughter all the days of our*
> *lives.*
> *AMEN.*

HAGAR

⚭

According to the biblical text, Hagar is Egyptian. She is Sarah's servant. When Sarah had not conceived at age 76, she followed the practice of her culture and gave Hagar to Abraham as a second wife and surrogate mother. Sarah complained to Abraham about Hagar's attitude toward her, and Abraham told her to do what she pleased with Hagar. Sarah abused Hagar, and Hagar ran away to the desert.

An angel found Hagar by a fountain of water and asked her what had occurred. Hagar told the divine messenger that she was running away from her mistress. The angel directed Hagar to return to Sarah and then announced good news that her child would become the father of a blessed nation: "I will so greatly multiply your offspring that they cannot be counted for multitude…. Now you have conceived and shall bear a son; you shall call him Ishmael, for the Lord has given heed to your affliction" (Gn 16:10–11). Then Hagar named the Holy One who spoke to her El-roi, "the God who sees me." Hagar then returned to Sarah and gave birth to Abraham's firstborn son, Ishmael.

Fourteen years later, Sarah conceived and Isaac was born. Isaac and Ishmael grew up together. One day after observing Ishmael playing with Isaac, Sarah became troubled and told Abraham to send Ishmael and Hagar away. Abraham was distressed, but God told him to do what Sarah ordered. So the next day, Abraham gave Hagar and Ishmael bread and water and sent them away into the desert wilderness. When their supplies ran out, Hagar prayed and wept. The angel of God answered Hagar from heaven. "What troubles you, Hagar? Do not be afraid; for God has heard the voice of the boy where he is. Come, lift up the boy and hold him fast with your hand, for I will make a great nation of him." Suddenly when she opened her eyes, Hagar saw a well of water. She drank from it and gave it to her son to drink. Ishmael grew up in the wilderness of Paran. Hagar found a wife for him in her homeland, Egypt (21:9–20).

It is obvious from the way God treats Hagar that she is an important matriarch. Twice in the desert God appears to comfort, strengthen, and lead her to a life-giving spring of water. In the first encounter she is alone and pregnant (16:7). In the second encounter Hagar and Ishmael are near death from thirst (21:17). Each time God saved her from death.

Hagar is the first woman who is visited by a divine messenger with the promise that her child would be blessed and become the father of an important nation. Like Sarah and Abraham, God made a covenant with Hagar and her descendants. Hagar has the unique honor of being the only person in the Bible to name God and the only woman in the Hebrew scriptures to see and talk with God (16). Why was Hagar blessed like Abraham, Moses, and Jacob who had visions or theophanies of God? The explanation, according to Elsa Tamez, is that "God wished to point out that the oppressed are also God's children, co-creators of history. God does not leave them to perish in the desert without leaving a trace. They must live to be part of history, and struggle to be subjects of it."[1]

Yet, according to the story, Hagar suffered exploitation and exile, and God sent her back to her oppressor. Why? Are there any explanations? Elsa Tamez thinks it is part of God's plan for Hagar and Ishmael's salvation. In order to claim his rights as Abraham's son, Ishmael must be able to demonstrate that he is the firstborn and had been circumcised. This would assure his place in salvation history: "Strangely enough Hagar gives God a name, the God who sees, because this God saw her oppression and offered her great plans for the future of her son."[2]

Miriam Therese Winter, in her *WomanWisdom*, raises two interesting questions that students of the Bible still wonder about today: "Did Sarah banish Hagar? Or did she give Hagar her freedom?"[3]

Biblical scholar Savina Teubal thinks Sarah gave Hagar her freedom. It was her deathbed wish. This process began with Hagar claiming responsibility for her child. Impressed by Hagar's courage in the face of oppression and a sense of her own spiritual power, Hagar—as Teubal concludes—is a model worthy of admiration: "Above all her close relationship with divinity and her inspiration to forge her own community must not be forgotten."[4]

Alice Ogden Bellis, author of *Helpmates, Harlots, and Heroes*, believes that Hagar's story raises the issues of the struggle for status between women and the ethical questions involved in surrogate motherhood:

> Hagar was victimized by surrogate motherhood, but it also provided the means through which she ultimately became the mother of a great nation. Are there other kinds of benefits, economic or otherwise, that might make surrogate motherhood an acceptable institution today, not only to those for whom it is a way to motherhood but also for those who are the surrogate mothers?[5]

In *Texts of Terror*, Phyllis Trible asserts that Hagar is an important figure in biblical theology:

As a maid in bondage, she flees from suffering. Yet she experiences exodus without liberation, revelation without salvation, wilderness without covenant, wanderings without land.... This Egyptian slave woman is stricken, smitten by God, and afflicted for the transgressions of Israel. She is bruised for the inequities of Sarah and Abraham, upon her is the chastisement that makes them whole.... All we who are heirs of Sarah and Abraham by flesh and spirit must answer for the terror in Hagar's story.[6]

Hagar is a symbol of the powerless foreigner who has been exploited, persecuted, or abused. Battered women, pregnant teens, abandoned refugees can find in Hagar a model of courage who discovers the Holy One close by in their desolation. As God spoke to Hagar so, too, God will speak words of hope and glory for the future of the brokenhearted and hurting members of humanity. The God who sees continues to lift up the downtrodden to high places. Perhaps God will involve us in this work of reconciliation. We can begin this journey toward healing by asking forgiveness of the "Hagars" of our society whom we know or whom we meet.

Hagar, the woman who names God, is a mentor for women (and men) today who are discovering feminine imagery for the Holy One in the Bible. The biblical writers realized that no human words can describe God fully. They used a variety of masculine and feminine metaphors for God such as father, potter, shepherd, mother, midwife, woman in labor, washerwoman, mother eagle, and mother hen. As we incorporate some of this new, yet ancient feminine imagery of God, we, like our biblical sister Hagar, may encounter God as "The One Who Sees Me." The biblical image of a mother holding her infant close to her breast may nurture our soul's longing for a comforting God. Women (and men) may realize for the first time what it means to be created in God's *feminine image* and discover a greater integration of the masculine and feminine in their lives.

REFLECTION

"The angel…found [Hagar] by a spring of water in the wilderness, the spring on the way to Shur. And the angel said, 'Hagar, slave-girl of Sarai, where have you come from and where are you going?' She said, 'I am running away from my mistress Sarai.' The angel of the LORD said to her: 'Return to your mistress, and submit to her…. I will so greatly multiply your offspring that they cannot be counted for multitude.' And the angel…said to her,

'Now you have conceived and you shall bear a son;
    you shall call him Ishmael,
    for the LORD has given heed to your affliction…' "
(Gn 16:7–11).

"So she [Hagar] named the LORD who spoke to her, 'You are El-roi'; for she said, 'Have I really seen God and remained alive after seeing him?' " (Gn 16:13).

"Hagar bore Abram a son; and Abram named his son, whom Hagar bore, Ishmael. Abraham was eighty-six years old when Hagar bore him Ishmael" (Gn 16:15).

DISCUSSION QUESTIONS

1. Comment on Hagar's suffering in the story. Was Hagar a victim of Sarah's abuse? Was Sarah also a victim? What role did patriarchy play in this story?
2. According to the story, Hagar suffered exploitation and

exile, and God sent her back to her oppressor. Why? Are
there any explanations? Do you agree with Phyllis Trible
that "All we who are heirs of Sarah and Abraham by flesh
and spirit must answer for the terror in Hagar's story"?

3. Do you think Sarah banished Hagar or gave Hagar her
freedom? Why? How do you feel about surrogate motherhood? Was it ethically acceptable at the time of Sarah
and Hagar? Is it ethically acceptable today?

4. Hagar is the only biblical character to name God. What
is the significance of this honor? How can Moslems, Jews,
and Christians, the spiritual ancestors of Sarah and
Hagar, discover common ground today through this story
of faith?

PRAYER EXPERIENCE

1. Breathe slowly and deeply for several minutes. As you inhale, be aware of God's love all around you, filling you
with delight, joy, and peace.... As you exhale, let God's
love flow from the depths of your being to all other beings....

2. Become aware of being in the Holy One's presence always.... Every sight you see, every sound you hear, everything you touch, smell, taste reflects El-roi, "the God who
sees you," and holds you close...

3. Realize that El-roi, our healing God, sees everything and
comes to all who hunger for wholeness.... Recall people
in your community and throughout the world who have
broken hearts, wounded bodies, brooding spirits, chronic
illnesses, tortured memories of physical, spiritual, or sexual
abuse.... As their names and faces come to mind, pray
that they may be set free and find fullness of life....

4. Imagine conversing with the great matriarch Hagar about

El-roi…about her relationships with Sarah and Abraham …about women in our world today who are abused and oppressed. Ask forgiveness of Hagar and the "Hagars" in your community and world for the injustice they suffer in our society—such as women who work in low-paying menial jobs, single mothers, political and economic refugees from poverty-stricken countries, and so on…. Ask this holy woman to be a mentor on your way to a deeper solidarity with women who are different from you, women who struggle for justice, freedom, and understanding in our society…. Decide on one act of empowerment that you can do together….

5. The Hebrew word for mercy, *rachamin*, is derived from the word *rechem*, which means womb. According to this powerful image, mercy comes from God's womb-love which tenderly embraces us when we come laden with guilt and sin…. Is there part of you that needs to be healed from shame or guilt?… Contemplate the light of God's womb-mercy shining in the darkness of your own and the world's sin…. Imagine God's womb-love filling you and the world with goodness and kindness…peace and justice…hope and compassion…. Imagine this womb-love spreading above us, within us, around us, and accompanying all the "Hagars" in our world through their struggles and trials, rescuing them and helping them begin again.

6. Say or write down a short prayer with your favorite images or names for God…. As you do so, be aware of how God's presence and love is revealed to you through this name…for example, "Father, I adore you, I give my heart to you"… "O mothering, nurturing God, kiss away the wounds of abuse in my life."… "Sophia, Holy Wisdom, guide me along the paths of justice and peace."… "Jesus, Healer of my heart, free me from resentment."… "O Cre-

ator of the Earth, open us to the wonder of tiny bugs and wildflowers."

7. Image God looking in your eyes, saying your name, and doing whatever needs to be done to transform you into a radiant image of God's feminine presence in the world.

MIRIAM

A t that time the Israelites were slaves working and living in oppressive, dehumanizing conditions in Egypt. Fearing that the Israelite population was growing too quickly, Pharaoh ordered a genocide to reduce their numbers. "Every boy that is born to the Hebrews you shall throw into the Nile, but you shall let every girl live" (Ex 1:22). When Moses was three months old, Jochebed, his resourceful mother, hid him in a basket. Courageous, big sister Miriam watched as her baby brother floated down the Sea of Reeds. Pharaoh's daughter noticed the basket and sent her attendant to retrieve it. As soon as Pharaoh's daughter discovered the crying baby, Miriam appeared and asked if she should get a Hebrew woman to nurse the child. When Miriam returned with Moses' mother, Pharaoh's daughter offered her wages to nurse the child. Later, Moses became Pharaoh's daughter's adopted son. As recorded in Exodus 2:10, Pharaoh's daughter named him Moses.

Miriam made connections between the women that would nurture Moses. She took a risk, spoke out at the right time, and brought together a biological mother to feed Moses and a compassionate, adoptive mother to raise him in a safe, supportive environment. Without Miriam, Moses' mother, and Pharaoh's daughter, the liberation of the Hebrews from bondage in Egypt would not have occurred.[1]

Miriam is the first person—before her brother Moses—to be called prophet in the Hebrew Bible. Earlier, Aaron is given the title in the context of representative of Moses before Pharaoh in Exodus 7:1. It is significant that the beginning and end of the exodus journey involves the prophet Miriam. Renita Weems notes: "There are other women such as Deborah and Rahab in the books of Joshua and Judges, and the Hebrew midwives Shiprah and Puah in Exodus, who may be classified along with Miriam as self-sufficient heroines."[2]

Along with Moses and Aaron, Miriam is a leader in the wilderness. The biblical writers regard Miriam as a colleague of Moses and Aaron. In her 1980 dissertation on Miriam, Rita Burns writes:

> The brother-sister relationship denotes parallel status in the religious sphere…. In addition, it can be said that, although the texts do not yield a single role designation of her leadership position, they do firmly reflect traditions which regarded Miriam as a cult official and as a mediator of God's word.[3]

Scholars think that Miriam was the author of the entire Song of the Sea, not just the first verse. She led the women in song and dance on the banks of the Sea of Reeds after the Israelites' escape from slavery in Egypt to freedom. "Then the prophet Miriam, Aaron's sister, took a tambourine in her hand; and all the women went out after her with tambourines and with dancing. And Miriam sang to them: 'Sing to the Lord, for he has triumphed gloriously; horse and rider he has thrown into the sea'" (Ex 15:20).

Later Miriam became involved in a conflict in which she and Aaron challenged their brother Moses' authority. Miriam asserted that God spoke not only through Moses but also through Aaron and herself. According to the text, God punished Miriam. Although God corrected both Aaron and Miriam, Miriam was the only one punished. She was struck

with leprosy. Commenting on the injustice of Miriam's punishment, Katharine Sakenfeld writes:

> The lineage of Miriam is a lineage of generations of
> women who have been rejected or humiliated for doing
> exactly the same thing as their male counterparts. But the
> larger biblical tradition presents us with another face of
> God, beyond the face of the One who puts Miriam out.
> The other face is of God who stands close to and defends
> those on the "outside," a God who has likewise been
> rejected, put outside, by people who thought they knew
> best. The starkness of Numbers 12 must not be under-
> cut but Miriam outside the camp may point us not only
> to the painful arbitrariness of her situation but also, how-
> ever indirectly and allusively, to the suffering of God.[4]

In Miriam's view, the prophetic call includes female and
male. "After all, as the prophet she has already spoken for
God at the sea even thought the Moses' bias would drown
her voice there," observes Phyllis Trible. "So now in the wilderness she seeks an equal sharing of prophetic leadership.
Hers is a commanding word, and the Lord hears it" (Nm
12:2c).[5]

Trible reflects on the meaning of Miriam's prophetic witness in Israel's history in a text found in Jeremiah. "Again I
will restore you, and you shall be rebuilt, O virgin Israel; Car-
rying your festive tambourines, you shall go forth dancing
with the merry-makers" (Jer 31:4, *New American Bible*). Here
Jeremiah recounts the exodus event and uses the imagery of
Israel taking up tambourines and dancing in the restoration
of Israel after the Babylonian exile. "Returned to her rightful
place, she (Miriam) along with other females will again lead
with timbrels and dancing. She participates in the eschatological vision of Hebrew prophecy."[6]

The story of Miriam in the Hebrew Bible begins with daring women who took initiative, collaborated in difficult situations, and became heroines of the tradition. These women challenged oppression, affirmed life, acted wisely and resourcefully in dangerous situations and threatening circumstances. They remind us that establishing connections with other women, affirming one another's experiences, acknowledging one another's struggles, and celebrating our sisterhood is indeed important work for contemporary women in our world today.

As a courageous prophet, a caring companion to her brothers, and a change-agent who led the Exodus dance of praise, Miriam is a woman who continues to speak powerfully, to people of every age, of the liberating power of God in our midst. Her story has been hidden for far too long. It is only in recent decades that scripture scholars have pulled together the bits and pieces about her in scripture so that we can remember Miriam, our beloved sister, and celebrate her leadership now.

REFLECTION

"The woman (Jochbed) conceived and bore a son; and when she saw that he was a fine baby, she hid him three months in an effort to avoid his death as ordered by Pharaoh. When she could hide him no longer, she got a papyrus basket, plastered it with bitumen and pitch, put the child in it, and placed it among the reeds on the bank of the river. His sister stood at a distance to see what would happen to him.

"The daughter of Pharaoh came down to bathe in the river while her attendants walked along the banks. She saw the basket among the reeds and sent her maid to bring it. When she opened it, she saw the child. He was crying, and she took pity on him, 'This must be one of the Hebrews' children,' she said. Then Miriam stepped forward and said to Pharaoh's daughter, 'Shall I go and get you a nurse from the Hebrew women to nurse the child for you?' Pharaoh's daughter said to her, 'Yes.' So the girl went and called the child's own mother. Pharaoh's daughter said to her, 'Take this child and nurse it for me, and I will give you your wages.' So the woman took the child and nursed it. When the child grew up, she brought him to Pharaoh's daughter, and she took him as her son. She named him Moses, because she said, 'I drew him out of the water'" (Ex 2:2–10).

When the horses of Pharaoh
with his chariots and their drivers
went into the midst of the sea,
the waters washed over them,
but God saw to it that the Israelites
passed through the sea on dry ground.
Then the prophet Miriam, Aaron's sister,
took up a tambourine,
and all the women joined in with her
with tambourines and with dancing.
And Miriam led them in this song:
"Sing to God who has gloriously triumphed;
horse and rider are thrown into the sea."

While they were encamped at Hazeroth,
Miriam and Aaron criticized Moses
because of the Cushite woman
whom Moses had married—
for he had indeed married a Cushite.
"Has God spoken only through Moses?" they said.
"Has God not spoken also through us?"
And God heard their complaining.
Now Moses was a very humble man,

one of the humblest on the face of the earth.
Suddenly God spoke directly to Moses, Aaron,
and Miriam.
"Come out to the tent of meeting, you three."
So the three of them went,
And God came down on a pillar of cloud
and stood at the entrance of the tent.
Then God called Aaron and Miriam
and the two of them came forward.
"Hear my words," said God.
"When there are prophets among you,
I make myself known to them in visions.
I speak to them in dreams.
Not so with Moses my servant.
He is entrusted with all of my house.
With him I speak face to face—
clearly, not in riddles.
And he beholds the form of God.
Why were you not afraid then
to speak against my servant Moses?"
And the anger of God lashed out against them,
And then God departed.
When the cloud had disappeared from the tent,
Miriam was like a leper.
Her skin was white as snow....
So Miriam was banished for seven days,
and the people did not set out on their march
until Miriam had been brought in again.[7]

DISCUSSION STARTERS

1. If you could ask Miriam one question, what would that
   question be?

2. How can women grow by affirming one another's experiences and acknowledging one another's struggles?
3. Miriam was a risk-taker and a dancing prophet. In what ways does the story of Miriam relate to women's roles in Church and society today?
4. Miriam was punished for her criticism of Moses' authority. How do women theologians, pastors, prophets, ministers suffer the same fate in the contemporary Church?

PRAYER EXPERIENCE

1. Become conscious of your breathing. Allow your breathing to relax your body. Try a centering exercise such as focusing your breathing, praying a mantra, or repeating a prayer word such as Shalom, Shaddai, Sophia, God, Jesus, Peace, Love, and so on.
2. Read each of the reflections slowly and meditatively. Open yourself to the power of God's liberating word.
3. Imagine you are big sister Miriam standing at the Sea of Reeds. The sun is warm...there is a gentle breeze.... Birds are flying over the trees.... Insects are crawling on the ground near where you are hiding.... You are keeping watch over the basket.... You promised Mother you would not lose sight of it.... Downstream several women approach the banks of the river.... There is laughter and chatter.... You hear water splashing.... You move closer so that you can see more clearly.... One of the women points to the basket.... Someone else wades over to the basket...picks it up and carries it back to an attractive young woman.... You recognize her.... She is Pharaoh's daughter. You notice the expression of compassion on her face as she picks up the crying baby and comforts him.... By this time you reach the place where she is.... You ask if you could find a

nurse for the child.... She smiles and tells you that this is a good idea.... Off you run to share the wonderful news with your mother and both of you come back.... Pharaoh's daughter cuddles the baby and then hands him over to the warm embrace of his mother.... On your way home your mother laughs...cries....and praises God for drawing Moses out of the water.... You jump up and down and dance around your mother and baby brother....

4. Imagine you are with Miriam after the exodus event.... You are singing...and dancing...perhaps playing your favorite musical instrument with the other women.... The celebration continues late into the night and the women sit in a circle...sharing stories...dreams...hopes...for the future.... Be aware of any exodus event in your life in which God delivered you from bondage that you want to share.... As you do so, be aware of what is going on in your heart.... Share your hopes and dreams for the future with Miriam and the women gathered around the circle.... Be aware of your connectedness...solidarity...and strength ...as a community with new freedom....

5. Now imagine you are Miriam, the morning after you have been banished from the camp.... Be aware of the sources of your strength.... Now reflect on your contemporary situation.... Be aware of any times that you have questioned authority and have experienced rejection or some form of "punishment" for your stance or activity.... Conduct a dialogue with Miriam about these events.

6. Invite Miriam to retell her story today in a way that makes her equal to Moses and a prophet for women in the twenty-first century.

7. With song, dance, poetry, or art, compose a prayer of appreciation for contemporary women prophets who are change-agents in our Church and society today.

A PRAYER FOR ZEAL

1 Implant within my heart, O God,
   the fiery zeal of a Jeremiah,
   the conviction of a Ruth or Rebecca
   and the zest of a Francis of Assisi.

2 Stir my slumbering soul,
   that it might sing a song of passion and devotion,
   drunk with dancing joy and desire for you,
   my divine and loving Friend.

1 May my heart be as hot as the heart of Moses *Miriam and*
   for all your children burdened by slavery,
   for all who feel oppression's steely heel
   or suffer rejection in an alien land.

2 May I, like your son Jesus,
   be consumed with zeal for you, Divine Beloved,
   for life, for justice and for peace;
   for all that I know in faith.

ALL Fill me with zeal, O God.
   Amen +

DEBORAH

In the Hebrew scriptures Deborah is portrayed as judge, prophet, warrior, and leader of Israel. She sits under a palm tree in the hill country of Ephraim. There the Israelites come to her to settle disputes and pronounce judgments (Jgs 4:5). The prophet and judge was well known for her wisdom and discernment. The Song of Deborah, one of the oldest texts of the Bible, describes Deborah as a national leader. "For Deborah arose, a leader arose as mother in Israel. Sing of women warriors, of Deborah and Jael."[1]

When warrior Deborah issues a call to battle against Canaanite oppression, Barak, the military leader of Israel, refuses to obey unless the woman prophet accompanies him. "Go," spoke courageous Deborah to the weak Barak, "the Lord, the God of Israel, commands you." Barak responded, "If you go with me, I will go but if you will not go with me, I will not go." Deborah speaks confidently to Barak: "I will surely go with you; nevertheless, the road on which you are going will not lead to your glory, for the Lord will sell Sisera into the hand of a woman" (Jgs 4:6,8–9). This passage refers to Jael, the woman who killed the Canaanite commander. "But Jael wife of Heber took a tent peg, and took a hammer in her hand, and went softly to him and drove the peg into his temple, until it went down into the ground—he was lying fast asleep from weariness—and he died" (Jgs 4:21).

Deborah combined the juridical, military, and political aspects of leadership. She is a judge, a prophet, a poet, and a mother in Israel. Scholar Mieke Bal writes:

> The function of the judge in the book is an integrative leadership function on a local basis, which includes judicial, military, and political leadership. In combination with prophecy, which confers religious leadership as well, the function of Deborah is extremely powerful. In sharp contrast to Sisera's waiting and confined mother, she is the instigator and head of the battle. She is the only judge who is also a prophetess and the combination is strikingly powerful.[2]

Some liberation theologians see Deborah's story as a breakthrough from traditional submissiveness to a more activist stance. Julia Esquivel comments on Deborah's and Jael's assertive stance in the face of oppression:

> The tradition of the strength of the male is broken. The captain of the armies of Israel asks a woman to accompany him into battle. And she who destroys the strong man of the enemy is a female fighter—Jael. She breaks a pact in order to defend the life of her people, its history and its future.[3]

For some feminists, Deborah is a model of female empowerment. For others Deborah's association with military activity is a problem. Jewish feminist Lillian Sigal expresses her concern with warrior Deborah:

> Her hymn to Yahweh gloats over Jael's tricking Sisera into believing she will help him and over Jael's assination of Sisera by driving a tent pet into his temple while asleep.... As we probe out holy texts for women to ad-

mire or emulate, we must be careful not to exalt the behavior of personalities who exemplify the values of patriarchy that treat the enemy as an "it" rather than a "thou."[4]

Gale Yee, a biblical scholar, believes that Deborah the woman warrior causes such mixed responses because: "It is precisely the liminality of the woman warrior, her anomalous position neither inclusively male nor totally female, that permits the metaphor to support, denounce, modify, or otherwise express various facets of gender meanings and relationships." Yee concludes that though the social organization of Israel would not have ruled out military leadership for women, it would not have been the norm. [5]

Yet, women were on both sides of the Israel-Canaan conflict. Deborah and Jael were on one side. Sisera's mother and her friends were on the other side. Writer William E. Phipps believes that at that time the worst humiliation for a man was to be killed by a woman. He notes: "The distress of the Canaanites is greater because their general is slain not only on the battlefield, but in a woman's bedroom."[6]

Even though Deborah is a judge, a strategist, a poet, a military and political leader in Israel, she is not referred to outside the Book of Judges. The bias of patriarchy ignores the contributions of women of God. Elizabeth Cady Stanton, an outspoken advocate of women's rights, expresses her outrage at how little things changed in religion in nineteenth-century America:

We never hear sermons pointing women to the heroic virtues of Deborah as worthy of their imitation. Nothing is said in the pulpit to rouse them from the apathy of ages, to inspire them to do and dare great things, to intellectual and spiritual achievements, in real communion with the Great Spirit of the Universe. Oh no! The lessons dole out to women, from the canon law, the Bible, the prayer-books and the catechisms, are meekness and self-abnegation; even with covered heads (a badge of servitude) to do some humble service for man.[7]

Traditional Jewish Midrash does not provide a comprehensive commentary on Deborah. However, what is present implies that Deborah's story raises some controversial ideas for the rabbis:

Deborah says Midrash made mistakes. Instead of going to Barak, her husband, she made him come to her, a sign of disrespect. The midrashists conclude that "eminence is not for women" (Megillah 146). They attribute to God the defense of their own marital vulnerability, adding wishfully that Deborah was punished by loss of prophetic power while she composed the song that speaks too much of herself.[8]

How do we react to Deborah? Do we see her as a heroic leader, a model of courage who, after twenty years of Canaanite oppression, led her people to victory and liberated them from injustice and evil? Do we see her as the wise judge and prophet who reflects the feminine face of God in a patriarchal society? Do we agree with Denise Carmody's assessment of her that "[a]t the least, this account reminds us that the laws constraining biblical women were never the sole determiners of their lives. When they had religious gifts or charismatic powers, women could muster considerable influence...."[9]

Or are we embarrassed by the justification of violence in Deborah's story? Do "women warriors" make us nervous? Can women ever exercise power aggressively? Are there some things, such as the liberation of the oppressed from injustice, worth fighting for? Or should women model a value system that stands for nonviolent resistance in the face of oppression? Perhaps, if we contemplate assertive Deborah deeply enough, we may discover new insights into her courage that will give us answers to these dilemmas. Like Deborah, women can become models of female empowerment who will energize and inspirit those who are held down and have little hope. The question all of us need to ask is how can we become the prophetic women and men that our world needs to lead the way to the fullness of justice, where all are one in the realm of God? If we want a companion to accompany us on this journey, Deborah will once again lead the way.

REFLECTION

"Then the Israelites cried out to the Lord for help; for [Sisera] had nine hundred chariots of iron, and had oppressed the Israelites cruelly for twenty years.

"At that time Deborah, a prophetess, and wife of Lappidoth, was judging Israel. She used to sit under the palm of Deborah between Ramah and Bethel in the hill country of Ephraim; and the Israelites came to her for judgment. She summoned Barak...and said to him, 'The Lord, the God of Israel, commands you, "Go, take position at Mount Tabor, bringing ten thousand from the tribe of Naphtali and the tribe of Zebulun. I will draw out Sisera, the general of Jabin's army, to meet you by the Wadi Kishon with his chariots and his troops; and I will give him into your hand.'" Barak said to her, 'If you will go with me, I will go but if you will not go with me, I will not go.' And she said, 'I will surely go with you; nevertheless, the road on which you are going will not lead to your glory, for the Lord will sell Sisera into the hand of a woman'" (Jgs 4:3–9).

D<small>ISCUSSION</small> S<small>TARTERS</small>

1. What impact did Deborah as judge, prophet, and warrior have on her society? What impact does assertive, warrior, prophet, judge, Deborah have on you?
2. How have women's roles changed in our society?
3. What models of female empowerment do we have today?
4. How can we be prophetic in our world and in our Church today?

P<small>RAYER</small> E<small>XPERIENCE</small>

1. Use some classical or instrumental music to help you relax. Close your eyes and take some deep breaths. Be aware of Shekinah, God's powerful feminine presence, dwelling among us.
2. Use a prayer phrase or a mantra to center yourself in Shekinah's strength within you.
3. Become aware of any experience of oppression that you perceive in your life...Church...world. Be conscious of any feelings, thoughts, sensations, images that emerge.
4. Imagine yourself doing battle with this oppression.... Invite others to join you in your struggle.... Be conscious of choices, discernments, and judgments that need to be made. Open yourself to Shekinah's presence empowering you to do what needs to be done so that justice will prevail.
5. Dialogue with Deborah—prophet, judge, warrior, leader. Invite her to accompany you in your battle. Share with her your thoughts, feelings, insights, images. Listen to Deborah's counsel as she shares with you some new insights and deep understanding into the oppression and injustices you face. Invite other mentors and companions to join you in this struggle.

6. Ask Shekinah to reveal to you ways you are being called to be prophet, judge, warrior, and/or leader in this situation now. Name, affirm, and celebrate your call in some festive way such as lighting a candle as a symbol of your call, or writing it down on a piece of paper and placing in a special bowl or container. Members of a group could place individual symbols in a container, around a centerpiece or candle. If you are a woman, decide on a specific way you can express your sense of female empowerment in your life and, if appropriate, share with others in your faith community. If you are a man, decide on a specific way you can support female empowerment and, if appropriate, share with women in your faith community.

7. Give thanks for the contemporary "Deborahs" who give courageous witness to God's liberating presence in our world as presidents, governors, legislators, judges, bishops, pastors, preachers, parents, relatives, teachers, journalists, scholars, theologians, coaches, counselors, health professionals, etc. Take a few minutes to say each of their names in a litany-like prayer of gratitude. For example: I praise you Shekinah, for _____ (name person) because _____ (name reason). If you want, affirm one or more of the prophetic women you know in some concrete way such as in a thank-you note, a phone call, a surprise visit, a small gift, a hug, and so on.

RUTH

The Book of Ruth tells the story of the relationship between two women from their own perspective. It is the only biblical text where the Hebrew word *hesed*, or "steadfast love," is used to define the relationship between two women. It is the story of female bonding between a daughter-in-law, Ruth, and her mother-in-law, Naomi. Naomi and her husband Elimelech and their two sons Mahlon and Chilon moved from their Israelite home in Bethlehem to Moab because of famine. Elimelech died, and the sons married Moabite women. Mahlon married Ruth and Chilon married Orpah. After ten years, the sons died, leaving their wives childless. Ruth decided to return to Israel with Naomi. In the first chapter of the book, Ruth expresses her profound commitment to stay with Naomi in one of the most beautiful passages in the scriptures: "Do not press me to leave you or to turn back from following you! Where you go, I will go; where you lodge, I will lodge. Your people shall be my people, and your God my God" (Ru 1:16). After returning to Bethlehem, Ruth met Boaz, a relative of Naomi in whose fields Ruth worked in order to support her mother-in-law and herself. Boaz expressed admiration for Ruth's loyalty to Naomi. (Ru 2) The remainder of the Book of Ruth describes Naomi's plan for Ruth to marry Boaz, Ruth's encounter with Boaz on the threshing room floor, the preparations that Boaz makes for the marriage, the marriage of Boaz and Ruth, and the birth of their son, Obed, who would become the grandfather of King David (Ru 3 and 4).

The Book of Ruth expresses the journey of Ruth and Naomi through loss, grief, and death to new life. Ruth and Naomi are two grieving widows who have come together because of their shared loss. In reading Ruth, Patricia Karlin-Neuman observes that

> [T]he God Naomi repeatedly names as the source of her desolation and bitterness is the God Ruth is prepared to embrace. Although she too is a mourner, Ruth is able to turn to Naomi's God. The feminist theologian Rachel Adler once commented that the power of the mourner standing up to say Kiddish Yatom, the prayer of the mourner in the midst of a community at prayer, is that the very person who has the right to be the angriest at God is the one uttering God's praises. And by so doing the mourner affirms the praise of God for others in the community. Ruth by declaring "your God, my God" makes God, once again, "Naomi's God."[1]

Ruth's vow is unique in the Bible. There is no other example of a commitment like Ruth's promise to Naomi. Her vow is made outside family, ethnic, and cultural ties. Ruth dedicates herself to Naomi because she loves Naomi. According to rabbinic teaching, Ruth's loving friendship with Naomi was rewarded with great blessings: "How great is the reward that accrues to those who perform kindly deeds" (Midrash Rabbah, Ru 11, 14). Mary Zimmer reflects on the close relationship between Ruth and Naomi:

> Her vow is not simple loyalty to a woman who has come to mean a great deal to her. Ruth's pledge is a commitment to another woman against and in the face of all the social structure and custom that most likely will condemn her to poverty as a foreign woman in a strange land.[2]

Biblical scholars Fewell and Gunn comment on the relationship from Naomi's and Boaz's perspective:

Perhaps she (Ruth) was recognized by Naomi as the real redeemer in this story.... Perhaps the gate of Boaz's people did come to consider her a woman of worth— like the woman of worth in Proverbs 31, a woman sub-servient and thus valuable to the patriarchy. Perhaps, they only thought of her as Obed's surrogate mother. Or perhaps, just perhaps, a few saw her as a woman of great strength and determination, a redeemer in her own right, deserving of her own story, a woman worth more than seven sons of Israel.[3]

The Book of Ruth reveals a glimpse into the solid founda-tion upon which female friendship is built. Ruth is the kind of friend with whom every woman can relate. As Renita Weems so insightfully observes:

The story of Ruth and Naomi is about two women who saw each through a lot, two women who walked each other through the good times and the bad: marriage, the death of husbands and children, relocation to strange lands, poverty, courtship, remarriage and births.... Each woman, in her own way and at her own pace, reached out to the other, nurturing when called upon, mother-ing when necessary, sistering when needed. They even-tually found the healing power of God in each other's love and forbearance.[4]

According to scholars, The Book of Ruth is also a subver-sive story. Ruth is from Moab, one of Israel's most despised enemies. After their deliverance from Egypt, the Israelites encamped on the plains of Moab. The Book of Numbers tells the story of the men of Israel having sexual relations with the women of Moab and worshiping their gods (Nm 25:1–5). From that time on, Moabites were forbidden from ever becoming part of the Israelite community (Dt 23:2–6).

Hence, for Ruth, a Moabite woman, to be the hero of the story and the law of levirate applied to her, which permitted an Israelite widow without heirs to marry her deceased husband's brother to produce an heir, was indeed outrageous. This law was intended to preserve Israelite families and property. In this biblical story, the leaders of Israel who wanted to exclude foreigners from the communities were being criticized. In contrast, Ruth, a despised foreigner, acts as faithful Israelite.[5]

Andre La Cocque compares the subversive way that Ruth and Tamar provide offspring for Israelite families from whom they have been severed: "Ruth is a second Tamar—foreign, childless, widowed, transplanted with the people of Israel, who like her model, goes to considerable lengths, indeed to prostituting herself, to obtain justice: the levirate marriage to which she is entitled. But Ruth is respected by the counterpart of Judah; she does not have to go through the shame of public denunciation and condemnation."[6]

In her reflection on Wisdom, the feminine personification of God in the Hebrew scriptures, Claudia Camp considers Ruth and Tamar "examples of the aggressive use of female sexuality in public places, which can meet with approval—indeed even canonical approval when done in the interest of preserving a valued and life-serving social order."[7]

Mieke Bal analyzes the story of Ruth from another perspective. She views Boaz as a wealthy, childless widower who fears old age and Ruth as a beautiful, young woman who transforms his life. Examining the seduction scene in Ruth 3:6–16, Bal concludes: "Ruth's approach is a stroke of luck that he (Boaz) would not have dared to hope for and, indeed, he is most grateful to her for she will help him out of his misery.... While Boaz gave what he possessed, Ruth gives what she is."[8]

Observing that Boaz's prayer for Ruth was answered by his marriage to her and in the birth of Obed, Murray D. Gow reflects on the blessing of the elders in Ruth 4 as a reflection of the divine will: "The prayer of the elders for Ruth's fertility is explicitly shown to have been answered by Yahweh's gift of conception to Ruth. The hints of a glorious future, contained in the blessings of the elders and the prayers of the women at the birth of the child, are all seen to be fulfilled in David."[9]

Ruth is a heroine for all women. Marginalized women in our society can discover in her story a source for empowerment. Women have in the past—and will continue—to find strength and deep love in their relationships with one another. As a model of *hesed*, faithful love, Ruth reminds us that there are no limits, no conditions, no end to love's power to give, forgive, and endure. She challenges us to embrace the growth opportunities that we encounter in our relationships with cherished companions every day of our lives. The journey of Ruth and Naomi through marriage, exile, poverty, loss of spouse and children to new life remind us to be there for one another and give of ourselves without counting the cost. When we walk hand in hand, and work side by side, amazing grace moves through us. Like Ruth, perhaps we too will promise another the ultimate gift of a God-sharing spirit—unconditional love: "Where you go, I will go and we will be together forever in our God."

REFLECTION

"But Naomi said to her two daughters-in-law, 'Go back each of you to your mother's house. May God deal kindly with you, as you have dealt with me....' Then she kissed them, and they wept aloud.... Then they wept aloud again. Orpah kissed her mother-in-law, but Ruth clung to her.

"So she said, 'See, your sister-in-law has gone back to her people and to her gods; return after your sister-in-law.' But Ruth said,

> 'Do not press me to leave you
> or to turn back from following you!
> Where you go, I will go;
> Where you lodge, I will lodge;
> your people shall be my people,
> and your God my God.
> Where you die, I will die—
> there will I be buried'" (Ru 1:8,9,14–17).

DISCUSSION STARTERS

1. Ruth, a foreigner, is the "heroine" of the Book of Ruth. As a Moabite woman, she was the most controversial character that could be chosen to help an Israelite. Who are the marginalized women in our society and what impact do they have on our culture?

2. Ruth makes her vow to Naomi out of *hesed*, faithful love. She decides to follow Naomi's God because of her relationship with her mother-in-law. How is the relationship between Ruth and Naomi like—and/or different from—relationships between daughters-in-law and mothers-in-law, wives and husbands, parent and children, friend and friend today?

3. How do our relationships with our close friends and family members affect our spirituality? How does our spirituality affect our relationships with close friends and family members?

4. What challenges and growth opportunities do you encounter in your relationships with cherished companions?

PRAYER EXPERIENCE

1. Take time to be still and relax. As you inhale, breathe in the saving power of God. As you breathe out, breathe out anything that keeps you from experiencing God's love for you.

2. Become aware of God above and beyond all names and images embracing you.... Use one or more of the following metaphors for the Holy One to help you focus on God's closeness to you...Mother, Father, Shaddai, Allah, Shekinah, Elohim.

3. Read the reflection from the Book of Ruth.... Be conscious of Ruth's courage and commitment.... Ruth, willingly, risked her future and let go of her past by leaving her native land and accompanying Naomi to a foreign land.... Be aware of a time that you took risk in a relationship with someone...made a commitment of faithful love to another person...ventured into the unknown.... Realize the love that you experienced as holy.... As each thought, feeling, image, or insight emerges, repeat, "holy is the love I experienced."...

4. Offer thanks for the ways you have grown as a result of this close relationship. Pray spontaneously, or make a litany of praise—statements such as "I praise you God for finding strength to go on during days we had problems...." Forgive yourself and the other person for past failures. Create a forgiveness litany such as "I forgive myself for_____(name failure) when_____(name situation) happened."... "I forgive_____ (name person) for_____ (name failure)."... Celebrate your love for this

person in some concrete way. Perhaps you may want to express your love for the other person in art, poetry, song, dance, or in a journal....

5. Ask God to reveal to you any challenges or invitations for growth that you may have in your close relationship now. Decide on one step you will take to bring new life, healing, and joy to this relationship now.

6. Name, affirm, and offer thanks for the marginalized women in our society who take risks and contribute much to our culture. One way to do this is to pray with your newspaper. Make a list of the women you read about, place them on your refrigerator door, and pray for them for a day, a week, or a month every time you open the door to take out or put food away. A simple prayer is all that is needed, such as "Dear God, this is your daughter, lift her up today." Be aware of any way(s) you can help marginalized women in your community, neighborhood, or church.

7. The story of Ruth is the story of one woman's commitment to another. If you are a woman, be aware of ways that you can celebrate your sisterhood with women you love. Invite a friend (or friends) to lunch and tell her how much you appreciate her. This may turn into a regular "sister circle" of mutual support. If you are a man, be aware of ways you can share yourself with women you love. Send a basket of fruit or flowers with a personalized message of affection.

ESTHER

⚜

According to biblical scholars, the Book of Esther, one of only two books in the Hebrew scriptures named after the Jewish heroine around whom the narrative develops, is either a historical novel or a vestal legend. This book is one of the most controversial in the Bible because it omits references to God. But its prominence comes from the fact that the story of Esther is a symbol for the triumph of justice for an oppressed people. From the ancient writer's perspective, Esther's importance is evident by the appearance of her name fifty-five times in this book—more than any other woman in the Bible. When the existence of the Jewish people was threatened in the Persian Empire, Esther risked her life and took courageous action that resulted in the reversal of an extermination decree against her people. Her victory gave rise to the feast of Purim, an annual Jewish celebration of the deliverance of Jews in Persia from persecution and death.[1]

After her parents died, Esther, an orphaned Jew, was raised by her relative Mordecai. She lived in the city of Susa in the Persian kingdom and was selected for the royal harem because of her beauty. After Queen Vashti refused to comply with her husband King Ahasuerus' command that she display her beauty before his drunken guests, the king became so enraged that he issued an edict that her royal position be given to another (Est 1). When Esther was presented to the king, he loved her more than all the other women and selected Esther to be the queen. When she became queen,

Ahasuerus did not know that Esther was Jewish (Est 2). When she learned of a serious threat to the existence of the Jewish people, Esther heeded Mordecai's petition to take advantage of her position and go to the king to seek intervention: "Do not think that in the king's palace you will escape any more than all the other Jews.... Who knows? Perhaps you have come to royal dignity for just such a time as this" (Est 4:13–14). Esther, daringly, agrees to risk her life to deliver her people from death. She replied to Mordecai: "Go, gather all the Jews to be found in Susa, and hold a fast on my behalf.... I and my maids will also fast as you do. After that I will go to the king, though it is against the law; and if I perish, I perish" (Est 4:15–16). As a result of Esther's intercession with the king, not only were the Jews saved from destruction by their enemies, but they were also guaranteed protection. It was written into the law that the Jews could defend themselves against their enemies (Est 5–9). The Jews in Persia celebrated their deliverance from massacre and named this celebration a Purim Festival. "The command of Queen Esther fixed these practices of Purim and it was recorded in writing (Est 9:32). Each year the Purim Festival is celebrated on the fourteenth and fifteenth of March when the Roll of Esther is read in synagogues throughout the world.[2]

Sidnie Ann White points out that Esther's having joined a harem was, in her historical context, a logical, reasonable way of acquiring power. Esther really had little choice in the situation; disobedience would have meant death for her and Mordecai. White concludes:

...Esther, precisely because she was a woman and therefore basically powerless within Persian society, was the paradigm of the diaspora Jew, who was also powerless in Persian society. Because she was successful in attaining power within the structure of society, she served as a role model for diaspora Jews seeking to attain a comfortable and successful life in a foreign society.[3]

An analysis of the characters of Vashti and Esther provides a rich resource for reflection on the challenges that wives of public leaders encounter in their use of power. Renita Weems writes: "The story of Vashti's reign stands as a valuable lesson about the enormous pressures, demands, and responsibilities upon women who live public lives. It is a memorial to the price often extracted of public women when they step outside of their prescribed roles." Weems goes on to comment that even today, it is unpopular to discuss women whose power was related to their relationship with their husbands. But she argues that some of the most significant contributions in history have been accomplished by wives of religious and political leaders.[4]

Also, Weems points out that Vashti may have prepared the king for Esther. When Esther makes a request, the king is more perceptive than he was to Vashti. This reminds us, Weems suggests, that

> We have a responsibility to remember, celebrate, and
> come to the aid of those women who once gave of themselves on our behalf, but who, for whatever reason —be
> it divorce, death of husband or political defeat—now
> no longer occupy positions of leadership.[5]

Mary Gendler suggests that women today need both Esther and Vashti as role models:

> I propose that Vashti be reinstated on the throne along
> with her sister Esther together to rule and guide the
> pyches and actions of women, combining the attributes
> of these two remarkable females—being softened by

grace, pride tempered by humility, independence checked by heartfelt loyalties, courage, dignity—such women will be much more whole and complete than those who simply seek to emulate Esther.[6]

Esther's story demonstrates how God chose a courageous woman to deliver the Jewish people. "Taking off her splendid garments, she put on garments of distress and mourning." Esther prayed to God, "Help me who am alone and have no help but you for I am taking my life in my hand" (Esther 4/ C:13–14, *New American Bible*). Marjory Zoet Bankson describes Esther's spiritual development as a transformation from "obedient servant" to a "mature and self-conscious woman in charge of her relationship with God. In a philosophical sense Esther was now ready to make ethical decisions because she knew herself. In a moral sense she could now love more fully because she could choose to give her own life to or for another."[7]

However, Esther's decision to risk her life did not remove her fear. She realized she could be killed, but she was also aware that God had chosen her. Esther opened herself to God's liberating presence in her body. Then she put on her royal robes and met with the king. As Bankson observes: "Her private quarters were like an extension of her body—enclosed, intimate and personal. She was able to open her personal quarters because she was centered in the cosmic presence of God, not in the particular place that was physically hers.... Her resources for influencing the king's decision were part of her own body—her beauty, her manner, her personal ties with the king."[8]

From her humble beginnings as an orphan, to queen of the land, Esther demonstrates how a woman can use all of her resources to lead a successful life in an uncertain world. Esther's use of her physical attractiveness, beauty, and persuasive power brought deliverance to her people. Contemporary women who want to succeed by working within structures in society and Church will discover in Esther a powerful role model to whom they can relate.

Pondering the richness of Esther's story can help women affirm and celebrate their female identity and sexuality. It also can challenge women to examine sexism in societal and Church attitudes and structures. There is much to learn from women who step outside their prescribed roles like Vashti and Esther, Eleanor Roosevelt and Hillary Clinton, Coretta Scott King, and Winnie Mandela. Their advocacy for justice and equality for women, children, and minorities has been heard around the world. Perhaps we should ask ourselves, how far have women come from the time of Esther and how far do women still have to go?

REFLECTION

"In those days when King Ahasuerus sat on his royal throne in the citadel of Susa, in the third year of his reign, he gave a banquet for all his officials and ministers. On the seventh day, when the king was merry with wine, he commanded...the seven eunuchs who attended him, to bring Queen Vashti before the king, wearing the royal crown, in order to show the people and the officials her beauty, for she was fair to behold. But Queen Vashti refused to come at the king's command conveyed by the eunuchs. At this the king was enraged, and his anger burned within him" (Est 1:2,10–12).

"After these things, when the anger of King Ahasuerus had abated, he remembered Vashti and what she had done and what had been decreed against her. Then the king's servants who attended him said, 'Let beautiful young virgins be sought out for the king.... And let the girl who pleases the king be queen instead of Vashti.' This pleased the king, and he did so" (Est 2:1–2,4).

"When Esther was taken to King Ahasuerus in his royal palace...the king loved Esther more than all the other women; of all the virgins she won his favor and devotion, so that he set the royal crown on her head and made her queen instead of Vashti" (Est 2:16–17).

"Then Esther spoke to Hathach and gave him a message for Mordecai, saying, 'All the king's servants and the people of the king's provinces know that if any man or woman goes to the king inside the inner court without being called, there is but one law—all alike are to be put to death. Only if the king holds out the golden scepter to someone, may that person live. I myself have not been called to come in to the king for thirty days.' When they told Mordecai what Esther had said, Mordecai told them to reply to Esther, 'Do not think that in the king's palace you will escape any more than all the other Jews. For if you keep silence at such a time as this, relief and deliverance will rise for the Jews from another quarter.... Who knows? Perhaps you have come to royal dignity for just such a time as this'" (Est 4:10–14).

"Then Esther said in reply to Mordecai, 'Go, gather all the Jews to be found in Susa, and hold a fast on my behalf.... I and my maids will also fast as you do. After that I will go to the king, though it is against the law; and if I perish, I perish'" (Est 4:15–16).

"As soon as the king saw Queen Esther standing in the court, she won his favor and he held out to her the golden scepter that was in his hand. Then Esther approached and touched the top of the scepter. The king said to her, 'What is your request? It shall be given you even to the half of my kingdom.' Then Esther said, 'If it pleases the king let the king and Haman come today to a banquet that I have prepared for the king'" (Est 5:2–4).

"Then Esther spoke again to the king; she fell at his feet, weeping and pleading with him to avert the evil design of Haman the Agagite and the plot that he had devised against the Jews…. Then King Ahasuerus said to Queen Esther and to the Jew Mordecai, 'See, I have given Esther the house of Haman and they have hanged him on the gallows, because he plotted to lay hands on the Jews. You may write as you please with regard to the Jews, in the name of the king, and seal it with the king's ring; for an edict written in the name of the king and sealed with the king's ring cannot be revoked….' By these letters the king allowed the Jews who were in every city to assemble and defend their lives, to destroy and to kill and to annihilate any armed force of any people or province that might attack them" (Est 8:3,7–8,11).

DISCUSSION STARTERS

1. In the Book of Esther, Queen Vashti, Esther's predecessor, refused to display herself before her husband's, the king's, guests. Why was this a daring decision? What price do women who live public lives pay when they violate their prescribed roles?

2. The Book of Esther tells the story of the Jews in the Diaspora who were a subordinate minority within a foreign empire, just as Esther was a woman subordinate to a dominant male. In what ways do contemporary women have access to power and decision making in government, corporations, and the Church? Are women's voices being heard in the corridors of power today?

3. In what kind of situations do women use their beauty and sexuality to achieve influence and success? Why do they do this? Have women come a long way since the time of Esther's attempts to gain power? Why? Why not?

4. How do contemporary women in professional positions and public life gain status, power, and recognition by working within structures? What are the advantages and disadvantages of doing this?

PRAYER EXPERIENCE

1. Slowly take a few breaths. Be aware of the air flowing through your nostrils as you breathe in and out. Let your body relax.
2. As you do so, become aware of the emotions you are feeling…. Feel them…. What joys are you feeling?… What feelings of peace?… What feelings of affection?… What feelings of fear or anxiety?… What angers?… What guilts?… What feelings of loss or sadness?…
2. Open yourself to Holy Wisdom,* Sophia's saving presence, as you read the reflection on Esther…. Be aware that Sophia will triumph over injustice…abuse…exploitation …evil and all that oppresses us…. Ask Sophia to help you discern how you can walk in the footsteps of Esther…. Be aware of ways that you can be a "life saver" for people in your life now…. Be aware of ways you can persuade others to help you bring comfort…healing…deliverance… peace…justice…to family…friends…communities… people in need, and so on.
3. Select an image, metaphor, word, or symbol from the story of Esther that touches you on a spiritual level.
4. Ponder its meaning. Dialogue with it. Allow it to fill you. Contemplate its richness.

---

*Wisdom is the feminine aspect of God and is personified as a woman in the Bible. Sophia, a woman's name, is the Greek word for wisdom.

5. Ask Sophia to reveal to you ways that you can, like Esther, make a difference to your family...career...church...other organizations and institutions by working within the structures.... See yourself doing something helpful...significant ... creative that will benefit others.... Give thanks for the women leaders such as Eleanor Roosevelt, Rosalynn Carter, Hillary Clinton, and so on, who have made important contributions as political wives and paved the way for women in public life today....

6. Allow a picture to form in your imagination that reflects the depths of your beauty.... Contemplate yourself as a beautiful person... a sexual person...a powerful person... a strong person.... Draw, paint, sing, dance, or express your beauty...strength...power...in whatever way feels most comfortable.

7. Reflect on yourself as an image of Sophia. As you do so, be aware of your feelings.... Open yourself to a new understanding of God.... Be aware of any new image(s) of yourself and God that you experience.... Contemplate the divine presence reflected in your sexuality...power... strength...spirituality.... Offer thanks for the beautiful, powerful, radiant reflection of Sophia you are....

JUDITH

$\mathscr{L}$

T he Book of Judith tells the story of how God delivered the Jewish people through a strong woman. Scholars think it was written in Hebrew at the end of the second or at the beginning of the first century B.C. Some writers question Judith's existence. Others, like Miriam Therese Winter, believe the Judith story could be based on historical fact. The question is, asks Winter,

> Was there a Judith? It seems more appropriate to ask why wouldn't there be? Her story is well within the realm of possibility.... Then why would a world, hungry for heroines, be so quick to dismiss her? Maybe because we fear she already exists in spirit in far too many women, and maybe because the violence of her act triggers a primal terror in males, that to succumb to a woman is to be vulnerable to death.[1]

The story of Judith is not found in the Hebrew Bible or the Protestant canon, but is part of the Catholic and Greek Church canons, which derive from the Septuagint, the canon of the Jews of the Dispersion. Like the Exodus story in which God delivered the Israelites from oppression through Moses, Miriam, and Aaron, so God delivered the Jews through Judith. The Judith narrative appears to be a reflection on the significance of the Passover celebration. It is the same literary genre as the books of Ruth and Esther.

According to the Book of Judith, Nebuchadnezzar is the king of the Assyrians and Holofernes is his general. At that time Holofernes controls many cities who worship the king as God. In one of his military attacks, Holofernes and his army, on his way to Jerusalem, surrounded the town of Bethulia and captured the water supply. The Jewish people after resisting for thirty-four days become desperate.

At this point in the story, Judith, an attractive, wealthy widow steps forward, with a daring plan to defeat the Assyrians and liberate the people (Jdt 8). After prayer and fasting (Jdt 9), Judith dresses in her most beautiful clothes and accompanied by her maid, travels to the Assyrian camp (Jdt 10) where she convinces Holofernes that she has fled from the Israelites (Jdt 11). On the fourth day, Holofernes invited Judith to a banquet (Jdt 12). Then, when he is under the influence of alcohol, she cuts off his head, and returns to Bethulia with the head in her bag (Jdt 13). As soon as the Assyrians discover the murder, they are overcome with panic and flee in every direction. The Jews kill a large number of them (Jdt 15). The high priest Joakim and the Israelites come from Jerusalem to congratulate Judith for slaughtering the abusive Holofernes and liberating the Israelites. The Bethulians conduct a festive celebration at which they proclaim Judith their heroine:

All the women of Israel gathered to see her; and they blessed her and performed a dance in her honor. She took branches in her hands and distributed them to the women around her, and she and the other women crowned themselves with garlands of olive leaves. At the head of all the people, she led the women in the dance, while the men of Israel followed in their armor, wearing garlands and singing hymns (Jdt 15:12–13, New American Bible).

Judith preserves traditions inspired by the Exodus event. By her example, she reminds the community of God's faithful presence which will deliver them from bondage. David-like, she, the weak one in the eyes of the male world, confronts the mighty enemy and defeats him through the power of God, who puts down the mighty from their seats and exalts the lowly. The complacent Bethulian leaders falter, but Judith assumes the responsibility for the community. She shows by her example the meaning of trust in God. Although her methods are unorthodox and confrontational—criticizing the religious establishment for their lack of faith, lying to the Assyrians, cutting off Holofernes' head, and refusing to marry —Judith is a model of faith and a Hebrew heroine.

Like Esther and Ruth, Judith demonstrates tradition undergoing change through reinterpretation. Each woman makes a contribution in a male world. No set of rules regulating females keeps them from being faithful to the covenant, and in the process they bring about the transformation of the tradition. Scholar Toni Craven observes:

> This woman (Judith) unequivocally declares the theology of the establishment invalid. Like Ruth, Judith knows a God who acts in hidden ways; unlike Ruth, she speaks openly and directly about this God. Like Esther, Judith uses her sexuality to her own advantage; but unlike Esther, Judith preserves her purity while still winning the favor of those whom she schemes to beguile. Of all women in scripture, Judith alone says that theological misrepresentations cannot be tolerated.[2]

Judith is an independent woman of means and a competent manager of a large household: "Her husband Manasseh had left her gold and silver, men and women slaves, livestock, and fields; and she maintained this estate" (Jdt 8:7).

Judith is also an assertive leader who speaks out for the public good. She addresses the leaders of Bethulia as equal partners in the covenant community: "Let us set an example for our kindred, for their lives depend upon us, and the sanctuary—both the temple and the altar—rests upon us" (Jdt 8:24).

Patricia Montley describes Judith as the androgynous person who uses both feminine and masculine strategies to achieve her goals. Judith combines elements of both seductress and soldier, attributes which are labeled in the West as feminine and masculine, respectively. The same Judith who so impressed Holofernes with her beauty and wisdom did not hesitate to chop off his head and carry it back with her to her besieged town in her food bag! (Jdt 11–13). Montley concludes: "Judith embodies, yet somehow transcends, the male/female dichotomy."[3]

As a new type of woman, Judith is subversive by demonstrating that a woman can be both hero and leader. She symbolizes all the biblical women that preceded her, yet she is a new creation. She does not require masculine protection. When the male elders shrink from their responsibility to come up with a plan for their besieged town, Judith has a daring plan to save Bethulia from destruction. Judith substitutes herself for the male leaders who are unable to fulfill their responsibility. Writer Andre La Cocque writes: "Judith substitutes herself, as a propitiatory sacrifice, to an establishment that has lost its head, much before Holofernes loses his for other reasons."[4] She is willing to risk her life and go where few would ever imagine. Just as Judith carried back the head of Holofernes and dedicated it to God, so had David done with Goliath. Thus, La Cocque reasons: "Judith is David in the feminine....At the time of the composition of Judith, it was surely not a trivial feat to feminize the hero of the day."[5]

A model for all people today, Judith challenges conventions and traditions that need to be changed. Like Ruth and

Esther, she breaks the stereotype of appropriate female behavior so that the covenant community could prosper. Like Miriam, she leads the community in a ritual dance of rejoicing. She is self-sacrificing, risking everything for the liberation of her people. She chooses a path that no one else has ever envisioned. As Alice Ogden Bellis notes, "Judith is a model, not just for women, but for everyone who would like to make an impact on the world. She teaches us courage, disregard for petty conventions and vision. Where these three abide, hope for a better world cannot die."[6] Judith is a woman of cunning, utilized for the freeing of her people from bondage. Surely, there are visionary women today, who, like Judith, are courageous leaders, clever and creative, who preserve the community, challenge the establishment, change outdated traditions, lead the worship, and risk everything to free God's people from structures, institutions, and laws that oppress . Maybe you know a few of these women. Maybe you are one.

REFLECTION

Now in those days Judith of Bethulia
suffered all these things.
She was the daughter of Merari...
She was beautiful in appearance,
really lovely to behold.
Her husband had left her silver and gold,
slaves, fields, and livestock,
and she managed a large estate.
No one spoke ill of Judith.
She was devoted to God.
When Judith heard the harsh words of the people
who were desperate for water;

and Uzziah's oath to surrender in five days
if God did not come through,
she sent her maid to summon Uzziah
and the elders of the town,
and they came to her and she said,
"Rulers of Bethulia, what you said today is not right.
Who are you to put God to the test?
Do not anger God.
If God does not help us within five days,
God can help us another time…
While we wait for our deliverance,
let us call on God to help us.
God will answer when God will…"
Then Uzziah said to Judith,
"All that you say is true,
None can deny your words,
for your wisdom and understanding
have been apparent throughout your life,
But the people were so thirsty,
they compelled us to make that promise
and now we cannot break our oath.
Since you are a God-fearing woman, pray to God for us,
for rain to fill our cisterns
so that we will no longer thirst."
Then Judith said to them, "Listen to me,
for I have come up with a plan.
What I will do will be spoken of throughout
    all generations.
Stand tonight at the gate of the town
so that I might go out with my maid.
Within those days which you have promised,
God will deliver us by my hand.
Do not ask what I am doing,
I can only tell you when I am through."

Uzziah and the rulers said,
"Go in peace, and may God go before you…"

Judith, in sackcloth and ashes,
cried out aloud to God:
"O God of my ancestor Simeon,
to whom you gave an avenging sword
for the evils accorded to your people;
they called on for help, O God,
hear me too, a widow.
You have been maker of miracles
to those who have gone before
and for those who have followed after,
well, here now are the Assyrians
who boast in horse and rider,
trust shield and spear, unaware
that you are the God who crushes war.
Break their strength by your power
and pour your wrath upon their heads
and give to me, a widow,
the strength to do what I plan
so that by the hand of a woman
their arrogance may be destroyed…
You are the God of the lowly,
helper of the oppressed,
strength of those who are weak and fearful,
protector of the forsaken,
savior of those without hope
God of our ancestors,
God of our heritage, have pity and hear my prayer."[7]

DISCUSSION STARTERS

1. Judith is a rich, attractive woman. She is an independent woman of means and a competent manager of a large household. Judith wanted her people to be free of intimidation and threat. Violence against women is prevalent today. Statistics claim that a woman in this country is beaten every eighteen seconds and raped every three minutes. How is Judith's agenda of personal security and freedom relevant for contemporary woman?

2. Judith uses both feminine and masculine strategies to achieve her goals. Patricia Montley describes Judith as the androgynous person who combines elements of seductress and soldier which are labeled in the West as feminine and masculine characteristics. Do you agree with her assessment of Judith? Why? Why not? Do you agree that there are feminine and masculine characteristics that women and men exhibit? Why? Why not?

3. Judith is a new kind of woman. She symbolizes all the biblical women that preceded her, yet she is a new creation. She is independent, not in need of masculine protection. She uses masculine and feminine strategies. She is subversive, a woman who is a leader, while the male elders shrink from their responsibilities. How do you feel about the kind of woman Judith is? Do you see similarities and differences between Judith and Deborah? Judith and Miriam? Judith and Esther? Judith and Ruth?

4. Judith is a heroine with a vision and a plan to save her town from destruction. She confronts the elders and, finding incompetency, is willing to risk her life to preserve the community. Judith's maid accompanies her on her journey. What opportunities do women have to support other women in changing traditions and conventions that are no longer life-giving in our times? Who are the contem-

porary Judiths, "the new women," that preserve the community, challenge the establishment, change outdated traditions, and risk everything for God's people? Do you know any women like this? Are you one?

PRAYER EXPERIENCE

1. In the stillness immerse yourself in the presence of the Holy One. Open yourself to the fullness of divine love. Be aware of any images that may come to you.

2. Find a picture of yourself and place it close to your prayer place.... See yourself as a strong, courageous, reflection of the Holy One...as a new woman/man.... Imagine yourself "acting as if" the Holy One dwells within you in everything you think...say...do.... The Holy One is acting powerfully through you in ways beyond your imagination.... You see yourself growing spiritually...naming and celebrating sacred traditions...choosing ancient truths... helping others...celebrating community....

3. Read the reflection on Judith slowly and prayerfully.... Be aware of people today in your life and in our world who are suffering from hunger...neglect...violence... homelessness... fear...poverty.... Fast and pray for their deliverance.... Join with others, if possible, to alleviate their sufferings in some way.

4. Imagine that you are Judith.... You die...go to heaven... encounter the Holy One...play with angels...and meet several women whom you have wanted to talk with for years...Miriam...Deborah...Ruth...Esther.... All of you sit in a circle...and have a conversation.... Each of you shares her own story...listens to the other women...asks questions...offers insights...makes connections...smiles ...laughs...cries...dances joyfully.... Each of you expresses

your own feelings about the most challenging…risky…and loving moments of your life…. As each woman shares, the group experiences a wonderful intimacy…and a deep solidarity with women of all ages…. You celebrate your new relationships in a beautiful ritual celebration…. Great rejoicing…occurs in heaven…and on earth…that day.

5. Be aware of the similarities and differences you experienced between Judith and Miriam…Judith and Deborah…Judith and Ruth…Judith and Esther…. Be aware of any images, thoughts, feelings, insights that emerge…. Record these in a journal, poetry, art, song, dance, or in some other creative way. Create your own ritual and/or celebration to celebrate your relationship with these women.

6. Get in touch with the "heroine" within you…. Reflect on the ways you have saved others from destruction…. Offer thanks for these opportunities. Remember with love the "heroines" of your life…. Offer thanks for them…. If possible, write a note thanking them for what they have done for you….

7. See yourself as a contemporary Judith…. Ask the Holy One to reveal to you how you are being called to be a heroic model of faith now…. Be conscious of how you, like Judith, can preserve the family and/or community in which you live from destruction…. Challenge the establishment that puts rules before people's needs…change outdated traditions that create obstacles for people on their spiritual journey…and risk everything to love and serve God's people now beginning with those closest to you…in your home…community…church…world….

THE SAMARITAN WOMAN

⌒

The story of the Samaritan woman at the well records the longest conversation between Jesus and anyone in the gospels. Jesus and his disciples were traveling through Samaria on their way from southern Judea to northern Galilee. He stopped to rest at the village of Sychar by the well of Jacob. The disciples left him there alone to buy food supplies. On this hot day, a Samaritan woman approached the well around noon to draw water. Jesus began the conversation by asking her for a drink. The woman was surprised by his request and answered: "You're a Jew. How can you ask me, a Samaritan, for a drink?" (Jn 4:9).

The woman was startled by his question because she realized that this man was a Jew. The Jews and Samaritans despised each other ever since the ten tribes were driven from the land when the Assyrians defeated Israel in 722 BCE and exiled most of the people. Some Israelites remained and intermarried with the Assyrians. This racially mixed group built a temple and worshiped at Mount Gerizim instead of in Jerusalem. They became known as Samaritans. They believed that they were faithful to the Torah and looked forward to the coming of the messiah. The well where Jesus and the woman met was located near Mount Gerizim.

According to the story, the woman questions Jesus about how to procure a bucket for the living water and about where the Spirit of God resides. Mary Zimmer, author of *Sister Images*, thinks the woman's process of questioning Jesus is significant:

The Samaritan woman has been judged as a cantanker-
ous and stubborn person, but her persistent, even sar-
castic questions, bring her to the realization that she is
known by this man at the well. She finds her Messiah
through her questions.[1]

Some scholars wonder whether the conversation between
Jesus and the woman actually happened. This story is not
mentioned in any other gospel. Mark's Gospel makes no reference to Samaria. The Gospel of Luke contains the parable
of the Good Samaritan (10:29–37) and the story of a Samaritan leper who gave thanks for his healing (17:11–19). In
Matthew 10:5–6, Jesus instructs the Twelve to avoid Samaritan towns. Scholar Rose Sallberg Kam believes that whether
the encounter took place or not is not the issue. She believes
it represents the Johannine community's faith in the authen-
ticity of the Samaritan tradition. She points out that this
story reflects

> the esteem the Johannine community rendered its
> women leaders, an esteem evident also in the Johannine
> conversation between Jesus and Martha (Jn 11:20–27).
> The Samaritan woman's true missionary status is estab-
> lished by Jesus' implication that the technical verb "I
> send you" (*apostellein*) applies to her as well as to male
> disciples; the writer also says the townspeople believe
> "through her word." This phrase recurs in Jesus' prayer
> for the disciples gathered at the Last Supper: "I pray not
> only for them, but also for those who believe in me
> through their word" (17:20).[2]

The story of the Samaritan woman demonstrates that
Christ is the "wellspring of love" that will fill us forever. Everyone is invited to drink the "living water" and belong to the

community of faith. Jesus' trademark is inclusiveness. As God's reign breaks forth in our midst, everyone is welcome. There are no outsiders. All that is required is that we worship in spirit and truth. As Rachel Conrad Wahlberg, in her book *Jesus According to a Woman*, describes the significance of the Samaritan woman: "Her culturally assigned status gave way to her Jesus assigned status—one who is worthy to go and tell."[3]

It is mind-blowing that Jesus confided his identity as Messiah and revealed who God is with an outsider, a foreigner, a woman living with a man who was not her husband, in fact a woman who had five husbands. According to biblical experts, the woman understood Jesus' mention that "she…had no husband not as a call to true repentance, but as a call to true worship. In other words, the exchange about husbands is not biographical, but a highly symbolic element within the theological discussion."[4] In the encounter with the woman at the well, Jesus goes beyond the social and religious taboos of his times. Jesus shares his identity with a woman who doesn't belong to the religious establishment and who is a foreigner and a divorced. For women, the Samaritan woman is an important role model. "It is impossible to believe that Jesus chose this bright, assertive messenger by chance," comments Rose Sallberg Kam, "when he could so easily have chosen a man. Somehow, in spite of all the negatives of her situation, he saw in her exactly the person needed to bring the kingdom to Sychar."

We might ask ourselves, what does this mean for us? Perhaps Jesus is calling women today to be leaders in the Church, proclaiming gospel freedom and equality in ways that will liberate and heal us from the bondage of sexism and patriarchy. Perhaps Jesus is reminding us that social acceptability and rule keeping is not what true religion is about. Jesus is assuring us that just as he filled the Samaritan woman with the "living water" of faith and joyful enthusiasm, he will do the same for us today. Like this gutsy woman, we don't need religious ordination, a degree in theology, or an official appointment to share Christ's love with people who are searching for God in our neighborhoods. All we need is faith in Christ and a heart willing to love and serve others. Maybe we should ask ourselves, what are we waiting for?

Now more than ever we need to proclaim by our words and lives that God is love, and that all people are loved and blessed by God. No one is excluded from the divine embrace. No matter how sinful, broken, or messed up our lives may be, God may be calling us to be messengers of divine love. Like the Samaritan woman with her checkered past, we don't have to have our act together. We don't need to be perfect—we need only to come to Jesus. This is what Christians for centuries have called prayer. Here we can argue with Jesus if we want. We can even ask questions, express our feelings or doubts, listen, or simply be with Jesus. Then, like the scene at the well, Jesus may converse with us, read our hearts, minister to our hurts, or simply delight in us for a while. As the conversation evolved, the Samaritan woman understood the spiritual meaning of Jesus' words. We too may grow more in love with Christ as we experience the depths of divine love flowing within us in our prayerful encounters. Like lake water sparkling in the sunshine, we will radiate Christ. We will become like a magnet—like Christ—to whom others will be drawn.

God calls each of us to share the love we have experienced with family, friends, strangers, and people we meet who are struggling, lonely, empty, confused, or alienated. If we say "yes," nothing else will matter. We will be an evangelist like the Samaritan woman. Isn't it time to leave our water jars behind?

REFLECTION

"Jesus, weary from the journey, came and sat by the well. It was around noon. When a Samaritan woman came to draw water, Jesus said to her, 'Give me a drink.' The disciples had gone off to the town to buy provisions.

"The Samaritan woman replied, 'You're a Jew. How can you ask me, a Samaritan, for a drink?'—since Jews had nothing to do with Samaritans.

"Jesus answered, 'If only you recognized God's gift, and who it is that is asking you for a drink, you would have asked him for a drink instead, and he would have given you living water.'

"'If you please,' she challenged Jesus, 'you don't have a bucket and this well is deep. Where do you expect to get this living water? Surely you don't pretend to be greater than our ancestors Leah and Rachel and Jacob, who gave us this well and drank from it with their descendants and flocks?'

"Jesus replied, 'Everyone who drinks this water will be thirsty again. But those who drink the water I give them will never be thirsty; no, the water I give will become fountains within them, springing up to provide eternal life.'

"The woman said to Jesus, 'Give me this water, so that I won't grow thirsty and have to keep coming all the way here to draw water.'

"Jesus said to her, 'Go and call your husband and then come back here.'

"'I don't have a husband,' replied the woman.

"'You're right—you don't have a husband!' Jesus exclaimed. 'The fact is you've had five, and the man you're living with now is not your husband. So what you've said is quite true.'

"'I can see you're a prophet,' answered the woman. 'Our ancestors worshiped on this mountain, but you people claim that Jerusalem is the place where God ought to be worshiped.'

"Jesus told her, 'Believe me, the hour is coming when you'll worship Abba God neither on this mountain nor in Jerusalem. You people worship what you don't understand; we worship what we do understand—after all, salvation is from the Jewish people. Yet the hour is coming when real worshipers will worship Abba God in Spirit and truth. Indeed, it is just such worshipers whom Abba God seeks. God is Spirit, and those who worship God must worship in spirit and truth.'

"The woman said to Jesus, 'I know that the Messiah—the Anointed One—is coming, and will tell us everything.'

"Jesus replied, 'I who speak to you am the Messiah.'

"The disciples, returning at this point, were shocked to find Jesus having a private conversation with a woman. But no one dared to ask, 'What do you want of him?' or 'Why are you talking to her?'

"The woman then left her water jar and went off into the town. She said to the people, 'Come and see someone who told me everything I have ever done! Could this be the Messiah?' At that everyone set out from town to meet Jesus...

"Many Samaritans from that town believed in Jesus on the strength of the woman's testimony—that 'he told me everything I ever did.' The result was that, when these Samaritans came to Jesus they begged him to stay with them awhile. So Jesus stayed there two days, and through his own spoken word many more came to faith. They told the woman, 'No longer does our faith depend on your story. We've heard for ourselves and we know that this really is the savior of the world'" (Jn 4:6–30,39–42, *The Inclusive New Testament*).

DISCUSSION QUESTIONS

1. Can we find God through our questions?
2. What is the significance for women in ministry today that

according to biblical scholars this story reflects "the esteem the Johannine community rendered its women leaders"?

3. Why do you think that Jesus chose a woman, not a man, a foreigner, not a Jew, and a divorced woman living with a man to reveal his true identity to and to preach the Good News of the gospel to the whole town? Are women called to evangelize today, like the Samaritan woman? In what way(s) is the Samaritan woman a mentor for women today?

4. The Samaritan woman was an evangelist, one who spread the Good News. How can Christians today minister with faith, intelligence, and enthusiasm? What is the good news of God's love in your life and in our world that you would want to share?

PRAYER EXPERIENCE

1. Take a few minutes of silence to become quiet and relaxed. Imagine that you are getting ready to dive off a cliff in the mountains into a beautiful waterfall below.... As you step of the cliff you float gracefully down into the depths of the water.... As you come up to the surface of the water, you float for a while on your back in the refreshing waters.... It feels so relaxing....

2. Now you decide to rest for a while, so you swim over to the edge of the water, get out and sit on a large log close to the water's edge....

3. You listen to gurgling of the water as it flows gently over the rocks...and watch the large fluffy clouds float by.... Foamy froth develops on top of the water as it shimmies down the mountainside.... The birds are chirping and singing in the trees above you.... You feel the cool breeze across

your shoulders.... You touch the soft green grass around you and admire the wildflowers nearby.... You notice rays of sun beaming down in a steam of light through the trees.... Everything feels peaceful.... You close your eyes and fall asleep....

4. You dream that you are a tree growing in the forest.... You bring forth beautiful blossoms and delicious fruit.... You send your leaves with messages of love and freedom to people that you care about...people from whom you need to ask forgiveness...people whom you want to forgive...people whom you want to liberate....

5. Slowly and gently you awaken.... You open your eyes and see Jesus sitting beside you.... He is smiling at you and calls you by name....

6. You share with Jesus from the depths of your heart.... Jesus invites you to do something special—something only you can do.... You are the chosen one for this unique mission.... Jesus looks at you with love beyond all telling, places his hands on your head, and prays with you....

7. There is something you must leave behind.... You give it to Jesus and say good-bye.... Feel energy and joy expand in your heart as you go forth blessed for your important mission....

MARTHA

※

According to the Gospel of Luke, Martha, her sister Mary, and her brother Lazarus live in a village near Jericho. In John's Gospel, they live in Bethany and are portrayed as friends of Jesus. The gospels record three encounters between Martha and Jesus. In Luke's account Martha protests to Jesus that she has to do the household chores alone, while her sister Mary sits at Jesus' feet and listens to his words (10:38–42). In John 11:1–45, Martha and Mary send a message to Jesus that their brother Lazarus is sick. When Jesus arrived in Bethany, Lazarus had been dead for four days. Martha went to meet Jesus and told him about Lazarus' death. Jesus assured her that her brother would rise again. Martha replied that she knew that he would rise again on the last day. "Jesus then said to her, 'I am the Resurrection, and I am Life: those who believe in me will live, even if they die; and those who are alive and believe in me will never die. Do you believe this?' Martha replied, 'I have come to believe that you are the Messiah, God's Only Begotten, the One who is coming into the world'" (11:25–27, *The Inclusive New Testament*). Then Jesus wept, went to the tomb, and raised Lazarus from the dead. In John 12:1–8, Jesus and Lazarus attend a banquet in Bethany which Martha serves and Mary anoints Jesus' feet with costly ointment and dries them with her hair.

Jesus is portrayed in these passages as a religious teacher who is comfortable in the company of women. He converses and eats a meal with Martha and Mary. He conducts a theological discourse with Martha on the meaning of the Resurrection. He reveals his identity to Martha as he did to the Samaritan woman. He broke the gender taboos, which did not allow women to serve or even to enter the dining area where male guests were eating.[1]

Martha appears in John's Gospel as a woman who takes initiative, gets things done, deals with her loss and grief, and expresses deep faith in Jesus. As Mary Zimmer puts it:

> Martha does not stay home this time, busy as a hostess for the funeral guests. She leaves and goes out to meet Jesus on the road, to confront him with the reality of her brother's death. Her first step to faith is the literal first step out of the house of grief and loss.[2]

In Luke's story Martha is overwhelmed, frustrated, and irritated from the pressures of preparing a festive meal by herself. Her anger smolders, and as soon as Jesus arrives she complains about her sister's behavior. Some commentators think that Martha was the older sister and may have owned the home and have been responsible for its organizational operation. One may be tempted to cite this story as an example of sibling rivalry, or as an example of a power struggle between Martha and Mary. Or to describe this story, as some homilists have in the past, as a vindication of the contemplative over the activist approach to life, or even, more inappropriately, that women belong in their homes taking care of their children and not in the workplace. Elisabeth Schussler Fiorenza thinks that Jesus' correction of Martha in Luke reflects the tradition of the later Christian movement in his time to put women in a subordinate position: "Luke's interest in subordinating one ministry to the other also comes to the fore in the story of Martha and Mary in Luke 10:38–42 where Martha is characterized as 'serving at table,' while Mary like a rabbinic disciple, listens to the *word* of Jesus." [3]

It is evident from the Gospel of John and the Gospel of Luke's accounts of Martha's story that both writers experienced a community in which women ministered as eucharistic presiders, preachers, and deacons. In Luke's church well-to-do Hellensitic women hosted the eucharistic celebration in their homes. But Luke describes Jesus reproving Martha and affirming Mary. Rose Sallberg Kam believes that this reflects a culturally ingrained male bias toward women, in spite of the witness of Jesus' treatment of women as equals. On the other hand, the Gospel of John was written at a time around 100 CE when the official roles of women were becoming more limited. Yet, the Gospel of John reaffirms Jesus' attitude toward women. What is even more striking, Kam concludes, is that the author of John "places on Martha's lips a profession of faith in Jesus as Messiah that Mk 8:29 assigns to Peter—and Peter's is a profession of faith to which popes still relate his primacy, and their own. For the Johannine community, Martha is thus identified as holding no less than apostolic authority."[4]

The gospels give us two different Marthas: the activist in the kitchen who is occupied with the details of hospitality; the confident, self-assured, and assertive woman who confronts Jesus about his late arrival at her brother's death. Do we need to choose one of these "Marthas" or can we choose both? Do the questions themselves draw us into a false dichotomy? For generations, the "Marthas" among us have been labeled busybodies, worriers, or even workaholics. Maybe what is needed is an integration of these two "Marthas" in our spiritual journey. It would certainly help us to be more balanced human beings.

Like Peter, Martha, a woman of faith, is remembered for one of the most important confessions of faith in the Christian scriptures, "I have come to believe that you are the Messiah, God's Only Begotten, the One who is coming into the world" (John 11:27). It appears that Christ treated women as equals and affirmed their spiritual gifts and authority. Like servant-leader Martha, contemporary Christian women and men are being called to a life of service in their homes, churches, communities, and world. Perhaps, biblical scholars like Elisabeth Schussler Fiorenza are right when they claim that the table ministry of Martha is associated with eucharistic ministry. If so, then what we need is a fresh approach to ministry in the Church in which women and men can celebrate their life in Christ as disciples and equals in ways that will witness to future generations the fire of Pentecost Spirit. One of the signs of hope in our times is the emergence of small faith communities, similar to the house churches in the early Christian movement. Here a new birthing of creative liturgical expressions and innovative forms of ministry are occurring. Wouldn't Martha be proud of us?

REFLECTION

"'Your brother will rise again!' Jesus assured her. Martha replied, 'I know he will rise again in the resurrection on the last day.'

"Jesus told her,
'I am the Resurrection,
and I am Life:
those who believe in me
will live, even if they die;
and those who are alive and believe in me
will never die.
Do you believe this?"

"'Yes!' Martha replied, 'I have come to believe that you are the Messiah, God's Only Begotten, the One who is coming into the world'" (John 11:23–27, *The Inclusive New Testament*).

DISCUSSION QUESTIONS

1. What is the significance of Martha's profession of faith? Do you agree that it signifies Martha's apostolic authority? Why? Why not? What implications does your understanding of this text have on the role you believe women should play in the Church of the twenty-first century?
2. The Gospels of Luke and John describe Martha differently. Which "Martha" do you identify with? What insights do each story provide?
3. Jesus is portrayed in these passages as a religious leader who is comfortable with women. Why did Jesus break the gender taboos of his culture and religion?
4. A grieving Martha meets Jesus on the road and says: "If you had been here, my brother would never have died!" Have you ever experienced similar thoughts and feelings in the losses of your life? How can our faith help us deal with grief?

PRAYER EXPERIENCE

1. Be aware of any areas of tension in your body. Relax this tension by alternately tensing and relaxing your muscles in those areas. Then starting at the top of your head, breathe in God's peace to each area of your body; your head, face, neck, shoulders, chest, abdomen, back, arms, hands, legs, feet, etc.

2. Journey to the center of your being and be aware of God's indwelling presence within you. Repeat a mantra, or short phrase from scripture such as "I am the Resurrection"... "Those who believe in Christ will never die"... "Jesus wept"... "Yes!"... or "I believe that you are the Messiah"... to focus your prayer and still your soul.

3. As you do so, be aware of times of struggle, loss, grief, or hurt in your life when you needed comfort.... Let your memories of people, events, and places emerge one at a time.... Choose one incident for deeper reflection.... You can go back and do others at a later time....

4. Be aware of your pain.... Feel it.... Dialogue with it.... Ask it what it can teach you now...where it can lead you....

5. Realize that Christ who is the same yesterday, today, and forever can comfort you now.... Ask Christ to do for you whatever will help you to heal from this hurt.... You may want to walk and talk out your feelings with the divine healer.... You may need to let your tears be your prayer.... You may want Christ to hold you close to the divine heart.... You may want to place this area of your life in a balloon and release it with Christ.... Stay as long as you want doing whatever you need to do....

6. Now imagine Christ giving you a gift.... You are amazed when you receive it.... You decide to share it with others....

7. You are aware that Christ is always with you and with your loved ones, wherever you or they may be.... Now it's time to go in peace to continue your journey of faith.... You are a new creation.... The power of Christ's Resurrection has touched you...and those you love.... Make your own profession of faith.... Express in it your understanding of the role you believe women should play in the twenty-first century....

WOMAN WITH THE FLOW OF BLOOD

✑

The story of a Galilean woman with the flow of blood, recorded in all three of the Synoptic Gospels, describes the sufferings of a woman who was afflicted with a hemorrhage for twelve years (Mk 5:25–34; Lk 8:43–48; Mt 9:20–22). According to Jewish cultic law, menstruation was a time of uncleanness and any discharge of blood from a woman outside her period made her unclean (Lv 15:25). Hence, for twelve years this woman not only suffered because of her condition which was related to her gender, but she was also cut off from relationships and activities with other people. Anyone and anything she touched became ritually unclean. Leviticus 15:25–30 states that not only was the woman unclean during her menstrual flow, but also, any man whom she touched was commanded to wash himself and his clothes. He remained unclean until the evening. On the eighth day after her discharge was over, a woman was required to bring two turtledoves or two pigeons to the priest at the entrance of the meeting tent. The priest then offered these animals in atonement for her unclean discharge.

The story describes her economic destitution and the failure of the medical professionals to treat her successfully: "...after long and painful treatment from various doctors, she had spent all she had without getting better" (Mk 5:26, *The Inclusive New Testament*). Luke, whom scholars think might have been a doctor, leaves out her impoverished state. He simply states: "[she]...found no one who could heal her" (Lk 8:43, *The Inclusive New Testament*). While in Mark's account the woman is talking with Jesus alone, in Luke's account "[s]he explained in front of the crowd why she had touched him and how she had been instantly healed" (Lk 8:47, *The Inclusive New Testament*). Matthew gives a brief version of Mark's account (Mt 9:18–26). (See Rose Sallberg Kam, *Their Stories, Our Stories*, p. 187.)

As the story unfolds, the woman approaches Jesus. "She had heard about Jesus, and came up behind him in the crowd and touched his cloak, for she told herself: 'If I can touch even the hem, I will be well again'" (Mk 5:27–28, *The Inclusive New Testament*). Immediately she was cured of her hemorrhage. After her healing, Jesus asks who touched him. The disciples are baffled by Jesus' query: "You see the crowd pressing in on you; how can you say, 'Who touched me?'" (Mk 5:31). But Jesus does not want the woman to be anonymous any longer. Too long she has suffered exclusion. Too long she has been unnamed—merely "the unclean one," "the bleeding woman." Jesus bids her stand forth as a person of importance—a Woman of Faith! She hesitates. Perhaps she has made Jesus "unclean"! But he hails her as a "faith-filled one"! By this healing action Jesus shows his compassion for the psychological damage she has suffered during those twelve years of ritual uncleanness. He heals her of the pain and shame of rejection, and at the same time repudiates the purification rituals of the law-bound religious structures of his time! Affectionately he calls her, "My Daughter," and praises her, telling her that it is *her* faith that has brought about her healing. The action of Jesus suggests that there is nothing unholy which God has created; and therefore, the body is holy— whether woman's or man's!

The context of this healing story emphasizes its message.

This cure is set within the story of a twelve-year-old girl, the daughter of Jairus, who is on the verge of beginning menses. A large crowd follows Jesus, Jairus, and the disciples. In the crowd a woman who has suffered a flow of blood for twelve years approaches him. Jairus, like the woman, takes decisive action. He comes to Jesus to ask for his daughter's healing. "My little daughter is desperately sick. Come and lay your hands on her to make her better and save her life" (Mk 5:23, *The Inclusive New Testament*).

There is a fullness, a ripeness if you will, in the very number "twelve." There were *twelve* tribes of Israel; Jesus chose *twelve* apostles because of the very perfection seen in the Judaic tradition in the number *twelve*. The twelve-year-old girl, just the age to begin menstruation, like the hemorrhaging older woman, receives new life. Elisabeth Schussler Fiorenza comments on the meaning of these stories: "The life-creating powers of women manifested in 'the flow of blood' are neither 'bad' nor cut off in death but are 'restored' so that women can 'go and live in shalom' in the eschatological well-being and happiness of God."[1]

Jesus touches the dead girl, and the woman touches Jesus—both making him ritually unclean (Nm 19:11–13). Like the hemorrhaging woman, Jairus has exhausted all his resources. Unlike the daughter whose father acts for her benefit, this woman takes responsibility for her own life and breaks the paternalistic barriers imposed by her religious tradition. "These two interlocking healing stories," observes Marie-Eloise Rosenblatt, "confront religious-cultic mindsets which prevent persons (the woman, the synagogue official, the household) from self-appropriating their own selves or enabling others to do the same."[2] In Jesus' time these two stories were shocking. "In a world where girls were chattel and where menstruating women were forbidden access to the well and the marketplace," comments Rose Sallberg Kam, "Jesus matter-of-factly summons two 'dead' women to fullness of life."[3]

The story of this risk-taking woman with a hemorrhage reveals a woman's dignity as a person in the face of religious and social discrimination. She is a model of courage, a shaker and a mover, who takes decisive action and assumes personal responsibility for her healing. Her journey to wholeness challenges her society's blood taboo. This woman of faith reminds us that when we reach out and touch God's power, miracles can occur that not only heal us but also transform oppressive religious rules, social taboos, and cultural norms. Surely, this woman's story is repeated in women's stories across the globe. So few of the world's resources are spent on women's health, education, employment, and well-being. Women and children still suffer the brunt of world poverty. Women and children suffer the most from the devastation of wars started and maintained by men gluttonous for power and territory. Women who do jobs similar to those of men do not receive equivalent salaries and benefits. In some cultures, women are subject to a brutal form of female circumcision, and baby girls are left to die soon after birth. Too many women are still second-class citizens and continue to be stigmatized for their femaleness by society. Into this scene, more than ever, both women and their oppressors need Jesus to come and set us human beings free! We need this bold woman's story to inspire us in impossible circumstances to seek our liberation and claim our healing: "If I but touch Him, I will be well again!"

In a world where pornography is big business, and women's bodies are exploited daily in the media, we need to appreciate the beauty and power of our bodies as reflections of the Holy One. Like the woman in the story and Jesus, women need to be emissaries of Spirit freedom. Let us shout it from the rooftops: "Our bodies are holy; we will not be used and abused anymore; we are free at last! We are taking responsibility for our lives and acting on our own behalf."

Jesus, who liberated the Woman of Faith, also, in his moment of dying, is pointed to as life-giving in the "outflowing of water and blood!" (Jn 19:34). Let us, then, praise the daring Woman of Faith in this gospel story for showing us the life-giving power of woman's flow of blood. And let us thank Jesus, the Life-giver, who puts right our jaded perspectives, who affirms for us our basic goodness, who pronounces us "blessed" in the face of our accusers, and who goes before us and with us into the eternal reign of God where all false values wither.

REFLECTION

"Now there was a woman
who had been suffering from hemorrhages for twelve years.
She had endured much under many physicians,
and had spent all that she had;
and she was no better, but rather grew worse.
She had heard about Jesus,
and came up behind him in the crowd and
touched his cloak,
for she said, 'If I but touch his clothes, I will be made well.'
Immediately her hemorrhage stopped;
and she felt in her body that she was healed of her disease.
Immediately aware that power had gone forth from him,
Jesus turned about in the crowd and said,
'Who touched my clothes?'
And his disciples said to him.
'You see the crowd pressing in on you;
how can you say,"Who touched me?"'
He looked all around to see who had done it.

but the woman, knowing what had happened to her,
came in fear and trembling, fell down before him,
and told him the whole truth.
He said to her, 'Daughter, your faith has made you well;
go in peace, and be healed of your disease'" (Mk 5:25–34).

DISCUSSION STARTERS

1. Reflect on the connection between the blood taboo and gender discrimination in the story of the hemorrhaging woman. Is this an issue today? Why? Why not?
2. This risk-taking woman speaks up for herself, takes responsibility for her life, and acts on her own behalf. What are the lessons you might draw from this story?
3. Compare the story of the woman with a flow of blood with the story of Jairus. What similarities do you perceive? What differences do you perceive?
4. How can people today break paternalistic barriers imposed by patriarchy? What fears need to be overcome in order to achieve this breakthrough?

PRAYER EXPERIENCE

1. Be still. Breathe deeply. Relax your entire body. Imagine relaxation flowing through your body from head to toe. Focus on each area and imagine your body letting go of stress and becoming completely relaxed.
2. Read the story of the hemorrhaging woman as if you are the woman.... You are sick, lonely, and exhausted.... Your doctors have tried every treatment, but all have failed.... Now you are out of money.... You have been abandoned by family and friends.... Your flow of blood has cut you off

from everyone.... You cannot touch anyone...and anything you touch is unclean...even anyone who touches
anything you have touched is unclean.... You are fed up
with the stigma...of being an outcast.... You refuse to act
like a victim of other people's prejudice.... You will not
let this disease define or defeat you.... You have heard of
a healer... Jesus.... You must meet him today.... You know
if you can only get close enough to touch his clothes...you
will be healed.... Energy surges through you.... You push
your way through the crowds, ignoring the people who
stare at you.... It has been this way for you for so many
years.... In order to accomplish anything...you have always had to speak up for yourself.... Once again you must
take action.... Out of breath, you finally get close enough
to touch Jesus' clothes.... As soon as you do, you feel healing power flowing through your whole body.... The bleeding stops.... You feel wonderful.... You are so excited that
you want to jump up and down for joy...but you remain
quiet.... Then you see Jesus looking at the crowd and hear
him ask who touched him.... The disciples look per-
plexed.... There is such a large crowd of people pressing
in on Jesus.... You hear people around you talking to one
another and speculating about who it might be.... You
wonder if they know it was you who touched Jesus.... Suddenly you are afraid...embarrassed.... Your heart beats
rapidly.... You decide to go forward.... As you walk through
the crowd...you keep your eyes on the healer.... Everyone is looking at you.... Finally, you are before Jesus....
You see in his eyes a love beyond all telling.... Jesus embraces you gently and says: "Daughter, your faith has made
you well, go in peace and be healed of your disease."...
Something happens inside you when you reflect on your
healing....

3. Be aware of any feelings, insights, thoughts, sensations, images that emerge as you reflect on the story of this risk-taking woman.... Dialogue with her about gender discrimination....

4. A woman's blood is sacred.... Reflect on the life-creative power of menstruation.... Contemplate the mystery of the blood that flows through you...that flows through women you love...that connects women with one another in every generation....

5. Be conscious of ways you can take responsibility for your life now.... Think about decisive actions you can take to experience liberation... healing... and wholeness in your life now.... See yourself joining other women to share your journeys together....

6. Reflect on the paternalistic barriers imposed by religion and culture that oppress women.... Write down these barriers, place them in a fireproof container, burn them, and as the smoke rises, let your prayer rise up to God, like incense.... Then sing or dance alone or with others in celebration.... Be aware of concrete steps you can take in solidarity with others to challenge these norms...rules...taboos...etc.

7. Compose a prayer, song, poem, dance, ritual, or artistic expression that celebrates the sacredness of women's blood —the power of menstruation.

THE CANAANITE WOMAN

𝒢

According to Matthew's Gospel, the mission of Jesus is directed to the Chosen People of Israel. The first example of a change in this direction was when Jesus released a girl from demonic possession at the persistent insistence of her mother. It was the impact of the woman's faith that moved Jesus to go beyond the limits of his mission to the people of the covenant. As a Gentile, the Canaanite woman was a despised foreigner, a pagan, and an outsider. Yet, she is the one who reveals to Jesus that his ministry is to the whole world, not just the Chosen People.

According to the story, Jesus enters Tyre and Sidon in southern Phoenicia. He has been healing people and confronting the Pharisees; his disciples have warned him of the Pharisees' hostility toward him. The disciples don't seem to understand a parable and Jesus has to explain it to them again. In other words, Jesus was not having a good day when the woman came to him shouting her request.[1]

The story begins when the woman humbly approaches Jesus with her heartfelt plea for her daughter's deliverance, "Have mercy on me, Lord, Son of David; my daughter is tormented by a demon" (Mt 15:22). Jesus ignores her. The disciples who want to get rid of this loud, disruptive woman advise him, saying: "Send her away, for she keeps shouting after us" (Mt 15:23). Jesus' response to her sounds negative: "I was sent only to the lost sheep of the house of Israel" (Mt 15:24). The determined woman, risking humiliation, falls at his feet and pleads "Lord, help me" (Mt 15:25). Jesus uses a metaphor to help the woman understand that his mission is to the Chosen People: "It is not fair to take the children's food and throw it to the dogs" (Mt 15:26). But the woman insists that the crumbs, the leftovers from his mission to the children of Israel, will be enough to heal her daughter. Astonished at the depth of her faith, Jesus assures her that her request will be granted. Her daughter is healed.[2]

According to scholars, the story reflects the debate in the early Church about how far the mission of Jesus extends. The words of the woman, who advocates table sharing with the Gentiles, not the healing action of Jesus, conveys the meaning of the text. The mission of Jesus is to all people of faith. Elisabeth Schussler Fiorenza comments on the intelligent, provocative retort of the woman: "She takes up Jesus' parabolic image of the 'tablechildren-housedogs' and uses it to argue against him." Her argument convinces Jesus and she has the last word.[3] This is the only recorded instance in the gospel when Jesus was "bested" in a conversation—and it is by a woman.[4] Marveling at her courage, Jesus gives her what she asks—her daughter is healed.

The Canaanite woman is an assertive woman who represents the despised "outsiders" in our world today. Audacious and sometimes offensive, she reminds us of our call to live the gospel message of inclusiveness: All are welcome at the table. This woman does not speak for herself, but on behalf of her sick daughter. Who are the "sick daughters" today, the outcast members of society for whom we would risk ridicule, rejection, embarrassment in order to help? Are we, like Jesus, at the point in our ministering that we need our perspectives stretched?

As an advocate for the "voiceless," she reminds us that our ministry, like hers, is to comfort the afflicted and to afflict

the comfortable. This calling is indeed as unpopular in our
society today as it was in her time. Perhaps as we come to
know this gutsy woman, we will discover the inner strength
that we need in order to be an advocate for the foreigners,
refugees, and the suffering members of our communities. The
Canaanite woman challenges us to question systems of
exclusion that separate people from one another in our society. We can protest budget cuts and lobby to raise the mini-
mum wage. We can insist on immigration policies that are
fair and just. We can elect candidates for public office who
will make laws that benefit the lowly and forgotten people.
We can insist that our country live up to the dreams and
values that make us all proud to be citizens, such as justice
and equality for all. We can make a leap of faith and embrace
the invisible people in our midst. Or we can reach into our
own pockets and financially assist someone whose education
and cultural background, very different from our own, causes
him/her to be caught in the cracks where social services do
not meet the need. Each of us can do something. Each of us
can make a difference. At our very doorstep we can find people
in need of many things: food, clothing, housing, education,
friendship, affirmation, financial help, and love. We can begin by getting to know their names and taking the time to
show we care. We can look into their eyes with love and a
smile. We can help the people in our communities who feel
abandoned and hopeless, to find work, housing, health care,
and most of all companionship. We can tutor a child in a
school, help the homeless at a shelter, work at a refugee center, talk to lonely people on a hot line, visit AIDS patients in
a hospice, support a child in a third world country, and so
forth. The possibilities are endless. As she challenged Jesus'
understanding of who he was and opened the way for ministry to all people, the Canaanite woman invites us to swing
open the doors of our hearts to all the "outsiders" in our midst.

Then all of us together will experience the inclusive, compassionate, healing love of God in our world.

REFLECTION

"Jesus left that place and went away to the district of Tyre and Sidon. Just then a Canaanite woman from that region came out and started shouting, 'Have mercy on me, Lord, Son of David, my daughter is tormented by a demon.' But he did not answer her at all. And his disciples came and urged him, saying, 'Send her away, for she keeps shouting after us.' He answered, 'I was sent only to the lost sheep of the house of Israel.' But she came and knelt before him, saying, 'Lord, help me.' He answered, 'It is not fair to take the children's food and throw it to the dogs.' She said, 'Yes, Lord, yet even the dogs eat the crumbs that fall from their masters' table.' Then Jesus answered her, 'Woman, great is your faith! Let it be done for you as you wish.' And her daughter was healed instantly" (Mt 15:21–28).

DISCUSSION STARTERS

1. The Canaanite woman reveals to Jesus that his ministry is to all people. Her argument convinces Jesus, and she has the last word. How are you like this persistent woman? Have you ever "won" any arguments with Jesus? Reflect on the impact of this audacious woman on Jesus, on you, on women, and on the Church's understanding of its mission.

2. This woman who was an "outsider," a despised foreigner, approached Jesus shouting for healing for her daughter. She made the disciples uncomfortable. Who are the "out-

siders" in your life that make you uncomfortable? What challenges do these "outsiders" bring to you?

3. Who are the "outsiders" whom the Church and society have ignored and/or ostracized? What gifts do these "outsiders" bring to Church and society? What can the Church do to welcome those in need of the Church's ministry today?

4. This woman pleaded for her sick daughter's healing. What abandoned group of people can you help? How are you willing to comfort the afflicted and afflict the comfortable on their behalf?

PRAYER EXPERIENCE

1. Become conscious of your breathing. As you breathe deeply, imagine tension leaving each area of your body and relaxation flowing in. Say to yourself, "I feel tension leaving my body and relaxation flowing from the top of my head, through my neck, shoulders, chest, back, arms, hands, fingers, stomach, hips, legs, feet, toes.

2. Read the story of the Canaanite woman slowly and thoughtfully.

3. Reflect on times either recently or in the past when you have been treated as an "outsider"...when you have been ignored...ostracized...abandoned.... Be aware of any thoughts, images, insights, memories, or sensations that emerge.... Write down a phrase, a sentence, or an image describing each experience.

4. Ask Sophia, Holy Wisdom, to help you get in touch with and express your anger at your exclusion.... Draw or write down, or make a list of your angry feelings and the causes or sources of your anger.... Express your anger by shouting, crying, running, dancing, drawing, writing, painting,

gardening, whatever. As you do so, allow yourself to feel Sophia's anger within you.... Allow this anger to energize you to demand healing....

5. Dialogue with your sister, the Canaanite woman, about her experience of being an "outsider"...a foreigner...a mother of a suffering child with no options left...willing to risk public humiliation...shouting for healing.... Listen to the wisdom of this persistent, pleading woman.... Ask her questions.... Share any insights or images that you have about her story.... Share your experiences of exclusion with her....

6. Reflect on the "outsiders" in your life that make you uncomfortable.... Offer thanks for the challenges that these people bring to you.... Be aware of the "outsiders" whom the Church and society have ignored and/or ostracized.... Ask forgiveness on behalf of the Church for these lost opportunities....

7. Ask Sophia to reveal to you ways that you can comfort the afflicted and afflict the comfortable...decide on one step you will take to speak out...to argue for...to be an advocate for...the abandoned in your church...in society....

MARY OF MAGDALA

A s the apostle to the apostles, Mary of Magdala is one of the most prominent women in the Christian scriptures. She comes from Magdala, on the Sea of Galilee. According to the gospels she was a woman from whom Jesus had cast out seven demons (Mk 16:9). We are given no description of the effects the demons had on her. Demon possession usually indicated some kind of emotional or physical illness. "Possessed by a demon" was a way to describe someone who did not behave according to the accepted mores of society. Seven different demons would seem to indicate that Mary of Magdala experienced intense personal pain. Whatever the seven demons meant, Jesus had healed her and she chose to become one of his disciples.[1]

According to Luke 8, Mary was one of the women who followed Jesus and supported his ministry with their resources. "The Twelve were with him, as well as some women who had been cured of evil spirits and infirmities: Mary, called Magdalene, from whom seven demons had gone out, and Joanna, the wife of Herod's steward, Chuza, and Susanna, and many others, who provided for them out of their resources" (Lk 8:1–3). Her name is mentioned first when a list of Jesus' female disciples is given. Scholars conclude that this means she was a leader in the female circle. Mary of Magdala has been identified with the sinful woman mentioned in Luke 7:36–50. There is no sound evidence to support this connection. Yet, for centuries many preachers, teachers, and theologians regarded Mary of Magdala as a prostitute, and artists and writers presented this distorted image of her. Some scholars claim that it was this identification that made the early Church leaders unwilling to use Mary's courageous witness as a model for women in the Church.[2]

Yet, according to all four gospels, Mary of Magdala is the only person described as being present at both the cross and the tomb. She is the first of the apostles to encounter the Risen Christ.

In Luke, Mary and the other women are present at the tomb; they tell the disciples of the empty tomb, but they dismiss their report as an "idle tale," and they do not believe them (24:11).

Matthew's account mentions that Mary and the other women were present at the cross of Jesus. She and "the other Mary" went to see the tomb on the first day. An angel appears and assures them that Jesus has been raised (28:5–6). Both women dash off to share the good news with the disciples. While they are on their way, the risen Jesus meets them: "Greetings! And they came to him and took hold of his feet and worshiped him" (Mt 28:9). Jesus instructs the women to tell the disciples to go to Galilee where they will see him.

In Mark's description of the crucifixion, Mary is described as one of the women who follows Jesus and ministers to him. She observes where Jesus is laid, and brings spices to the tomb after the Sabbath. When Jesus rises, he appears first to Mary of Magdala who proceeds to tell the disciples. They do not believe her.

According to the Gospel of John, Mary of Magdala is alone when she approaches the tomb early in the morning, while it was still dark. Observing that the stone had been rolled away from the entrance, she ran and reported to Peter and the disciple whom Jesus loved: "The Rabbi has been taken from the tomb! We don't know where they have put him!" (Jn 20:2, *The Inclusive New Testament*). The disciples ran to the tomb, looked in, and saw the linen wrappings there. Then they returned home.

But Mary stayed outside the tomb, weeping. As she looked into the tomb, she saw two angels in dazzling robes. They asked her why she was weeping. She replied: "Because they have taken away my Rabbi, and I don't know where they have put him" (Jn 20:13). No sooner had she said this, than she turned around to see Jesus standing there, but she didn't recognize him. She thought it was the gardener. Mary asked if he had taken away the body. Jesus said her name, "Mary!" She turned to him and said, "Rabboni!"—which means "Teacher" (Jn 20:16). Then Mary went to the disciples and shared what Jesus had said to her (Jn 20:18).[3]

The Gospel of John describes a close relationship between Mary of Magdala and Jesus. When the other disciples come and go, Mary stays near by, weeping, searching for clues of Jesus' whereabouts. Her grief is real. She has listened to his teaching and experienced his healing love. This type of deep friendship suggests a break with the social conventions of the time. Jesus regards Mary as an equal among the male disciples and, in an age when a woman's word was suspect, calls her to be the apostle to the apostles.[4]

In a third-century writing, *Pistis Sophia*, Jesus chooses Mary of Magdala and John to "be on my right and on my left and I am they and they are I." Mary's prominence is reflected throughout this document. She asks 39 out of 46 questions and participates in providing interpretation in this document. Peter expresses resentment toward her throughout the work: "My Lord, we shall not be able to endure this woman, for she takes our opportunity and she has not let any of us speak but talks all the time herself." Mary objects to Peter's efforts to intimidate her and charges that he "hates the female race."[5] Mary holds firm to her conviction that women or men who received revelations have an obligation to speak. "The argument between Peter and Mary Magdalene," comments Elisabeth Schussler Fiorenza, "reflects the debate in the early Church on whether women are the legitimate transmitters of apostolic revelation and tradition." [6]

Raymond E. Brown observes that the tradition that Jesus appeared first to Mary Magdalene is probably historical:

> A key to Peter's importance in the apostolate was the tradition that he was the first to see the risen Jesus (1 Cor 15:5, Lk 24:34). More than any other gospel, John revises this tradition about Peter.... In John (and in Matthew) Mary Magdalene is sent by the risen Lord.... True, this is not a mission to the whole world, but Mary Magdalene comes close to meeting the basic Pauline requirements of an apostle; and it is she, not Peter, who is the first to see the risen Jesus....[7]

In conclusion, Mary of Magdala was a close friend and disciple of Jesus. She is sent by Christ to witness to the male apostles. Even though she experienced disbelief and hostility from them, she persisted in her mission to proclaim the Easter event. According to Church tradition she is the apostle to the apostles.[8] The courageous witness of Mary of Magdala gives hope to women in the Church today who are working for the transformation of patriarchy and for the inclusion of women in all the Church's ministries. Perhaps the question that needs to be asked is when will the Church treat women like Jesus did—as disciples and equals—called to be partners in the proclamation of the gospel?

REFLECTION

"Meanwhile, Mary stood weeping beside the tomb. Even as she wept, she stooped to peer inside, and there she saw two angels in dazzling robes. One was seated at the head and the other at the foot of the place where Jesus' body had lain.

"They asked her, 'Why are you weeping?'

"She answered them, 'Because they have taken away my Rabbi, and I don't know where they have put him.'

"No sooner had she said this, than she turned around and caught sight of Jesus standing there, but she didn't know it was Jesus. He asked her 'why are you weeping! For whom are you looking?'

"She supposed it was the gardener, so she said, 'Please, if you're the one who carried him away, tell me where you've laid him and I will take him away.'

"Jesus said to her, 'Mary!'

"She turned to him and said, 'Rabboni!'—which means 'Teacher.'

"Jesus then said, 'Don't hold on to me, for I have not yet ascended to Abba God. Rather, go to the sisters and brothers and tell them 'I'm ascending to my Abba and to your Abba, my God and your God!'

"Then Mary went to the disciples. 'I have seen the Teacher!' she announced. Then she reported what he had said to her" (Jn 20:13–18).[9]

A noncanonical source, the Gospel of Philip, describes Mary as a target of criticism and envy for the other disciples: "...the companion of the [Savior], Mary Magdalene. [But Christ loved] her more than [all] the disciples. They said to him, 'Why do you love her more than all of us?' The Savior answered and said to them, 'Why do I not love you as (Love) her?'" (Gospel of Philip 63:32—64:5).[10]

In another noncanonical source, the Gospel of Mary, Mary

of Magdala tells the disciples to proclaim the gospel without fear. She assures them of the Savior's presence. In the second part she shares a vision she has received. Peter and Andrew react with scorn to her revelations, but Levi defends her:

> Peter, thou hast ever been of hasty temper. Now I see thou dost exercise thyself against the woman like the adversaries. But if the Savior has made her worthy, who then art thou to reject her? Certainly the Savior knows her surely enough. Let us rather be ashamed, put on the perfect man, as he has charged us, and proclaim the Gospel.[11]

DISCUSSION STARTERS

1. The Gospel of John gives evidence of a close friendship between Mary of Magdala and Jesus. This kind of relationship would indicate a clear break with Judaic custom. How is this relationship a model for women and men in ministry today?

2. Jesus treats Mary as an equal among the disciples. What impact did Jesus' attitude and treatment of women in the gospels have on Church teaching and practice through the centuries?

3. According to some noncanonical sources there was hostility between Mary of Magdala and Peter. How do Church officials today respond to women's issues? What is your reaction to the current debate about women's roles in the Church today?

4. What challenges do you face in proclaiming the gospel with courage and conviction today? What challenges do women face in proclaiming the gospel with courage and conviction today?

PRAYER EXPERIENCE

1. Make yourself comfortable and take several slow, deep breaths. Where there is muscle tension, let go. Look at your surroundings with awe and wonder, like a baby seeing the world for the first time. As you do so, be conscious of how each person/place/thing reflects the love of the Risen Christ.

2. Be aware of a time of grief or personal loss in your life…. You have lost a loved one(s)…. You are overcome with grief…. You don't know what to do…. Suddenly you sense a presence near you…. You don't know who it is…. A voice asks you…"Why are you weeping?"… You name your loss(es) and share your pain…. Suddenly you become aware that Christ is with you…. You rest in the embrace of the Risen One…. Christ looks into your eyes…comforts you…fills you with peace…assures you that your loved one(s) is happy…and one day you will be together…. The Risen One invites you to celebrate this person's life (these persons' lives) in a special way today…. You know exactly how you will do this…. Now is the time to live fully and love deeply….

2. Imagine you could interview Mary of Magdala about her encounter with the Risen Christ and her experiences with the male disciples after the Resurrection…. What questions would you ask her?… How do you think she would respond?…

3. Now imagine that Mary of Magdala is present at a Vatican Council called to address women's roles in the Church in the twenty-first century. Be aware of any questions… comments…observations…revelations…feelings…insights …she might share. Be aware of any responses she might receive from Vatican officials…Church members…news media…etc.

4. Invite Mary of Magdala to dialogue with the pope and bishops of the Roman Catholic Church on the role of women in the Church from the perspective of her relationship with Christ, her relationships with the male disciples, and her call to be apostle to the apostles.

5. Invite Mary of Magdala to dialogue with contemporary feminist theologians, and/or to meet with a women's spirituality group. Observe the questions, thoughts, insights, observations, prayer rituals, celebrations that emerge.

6. Invite the Risen Christ to reveal to you any new ways you can proclaim the Easter event in your life. Pray your own or any of the following mantras that express the Risen Christ's love for you:

> "I have called you by name."
> "You are my beloved."
> "I will always love you."
> "I will wipe away your tears."
> "I will comfort you."

7. Record your responses to the above prayer experiences in a journal, poetry, drama, art, song, dance, or in some other creative way.

WOMAN WHO ANOINTS JESUS' HEAD

⌇

The story of the woman who anoints Jesus is told in all four gospels. In Mark and Matthew, the anointing occurs at the home of Simon the leper in Bethany. In Luke, the place is unknown, and Simon becomes a Pharisee. In John, the location is the home of Martha in Bethany. In Mark and Matthew, the head of Jesus is anointed; in Luke and John his feet are anointed. According to Mark, Matthew, and John, the meaning of the story is the anointing of Jesus' body before burial. There are three different women in these accounts. In John's Gospel the woman is identified as Mary of Bethany, a close friend of Jesus. Luke changes the identity of the woman from disciple to sinner and the focus is on forgiveness of a sinful woman.[1]

The passion narrative of Mark's Gospel provides the context for the story of the woman who anoints Jesus. It takes place two days before the Passover. In the preceding chapter Jesus had instructed his disciples to "keep alert." The verse before the story of the woman describes the plot of the religious leaders to kill Jesus. The passage after this story describes Judas' meeting with the chief priests to plan the betrayal of Jesus. Later in the passion narrative Mark tells the story of Peter's denial. It is evident from Mark's perspective that the male disciples don't comprehend that suffering is part of the mission of Jesus. Its significance escapes them. They reject the suffering Messiah and, in the end, abandon or betray him. However, the female disciples who have journeyed with the Messiah from Galilee to Jerusalem become the true disciples of Jesus. The prophet in the Hebrew scriptures anointed the head of the Jewish king; the anointing of Jesus' head must have indicated the prophetic recognition of Jesus. It was a woman who named Jesus by her prophetic action. "The un-named woman who names Jesus with a prophetic sign-action in Mark's Gospel," observes Elisabeth Schussler Fiorenza, "is the paradigm for the true disciple....This is a politically dangerous story. While Peter has confessed, without truly understanding it, 'you are the anointed one,' the woman anointing Jesus recognizes clearly that Jesus' messiahship means suffering and death."[2] Jesus affirms the woman's prophetic gesture for all time, "Truly I tell you, wherever the good news is proclaimed in the whole world, what she has done will be told in remembrance of her" (Mk 14:9).

Even the outrage of the male disciples did not stop her from pouring forth her gift. Jesus clearly defends her bold actions and reproves the men who criticize her for her extravagant waste of money which they claimed could have been used to help the poor.[3] He contrasts the extravagant love of the woman with their insensitivity. "Let her alone; why do you trouble her? She has performed a good service for me. For you always have the poor with you, and you can show kindness to them whenever you wish; but you will not always have me" (Mk 14:6–7). Intuitively, this woman knows that Jesus is the Christ. When she breaks open the jar of costly ointment and pours the ointment on his head, she breaks through societal norms and overcomes false perceptions about what was important at that time. Jesus' response to the anointing was to give her a prominent place as a faithful disciple and model for all Christians—wherever the gospel is proclaimed, she will be remembered.[4]

It is a sad testimony to patriarchy's influence that in spite of Jesus' words, Christians throughout the ages have forgotten this courageous woman. Her sacred testimony has been ignored. It is striking that the Spirit of God inspires a simple, unnamed woman, one of the ordinary, average people who form the larger circle of followers of Jesus, to be the anointer of the Messiah and prophet of the sacrificial nature of his messiahship. Ordinarily, in the customs of the day, it would be unheard of for anyone besides a priest or prophet, usually male, to preside at a public anointing. Yet, here she comes in her simplicity, in spite of the hostility and criticism of the disciples, to pour her vial of precious oil on his head.

This prophetic woman challenges us to risk everything in order to share our gifts. She also challenges us to listen to the urgings of the Holy Spirit in our lives, for the Spirit does at times move us to the unpopular, more daring public action. Like her, we do what we can do—but whatever it is, it amounts to pouring out the extravagance of our love on others. Like her, we can break through the arrogance and fury of those who don't understand, and anoint Jesus, the Christ who dies and rises each day in women and men everywhere. We can reclaim for woman her position in the tradition as Christian ministers and witnesses. In prayer we can dialogue with these powerful icons of the faith. Then, when the gospel is proclaimed, we will remember and celebrate woman-strength, woman-passion, woman-wisdom, woman-truth and, woman-courage!

REFLECTION

"While he was at Bethany in the house of Simon the leper, as he sat at the table, a woman came with an alabaster jar of very costly ointment of nard, and she broke open the jar and poured the ointment on his head. But some were there who said to one another in anger, 'Why was the ointment wasted in this way? For this ointment could have been sold for more than 300 denarii, and the money given to the poor.' And they scolded her. But Jesus said, 'Let her alone; why do you trouble her? She has performed a good service for me. For you always have the poor with you, and you can show kindness to them whenever you wish; but you will not always have me. She has done what she could; she has anointed my body beforehand for its burial. Truly, I tell you, wherever the good news is proclaimed in the whole world, what she has done will be told in remembrance of her'" (Mk 14:3–9).

DISCUSSION STARTERS

1. Once again we read about an unnamed woman in the gospels who has been forgotten. Why is it important that we reclaim women in the tradition as Christian ministers and witnesses?

2. Christian feminist theology and biblical interpretation is rediscovering that the gospel cannot be proclaimed unless women disciples are remembered. How can Christian feminist theology and biblical studies help us remember women in the tradition? What can you do to make this happen?

3. According to Elizabeth Schussler Fiorenza's groundbreaking book, *In Memory of Her*, the anointing of Jesus' head was understood as a prophetic recognition of Jesus, the Christ, the Messiah. This was a politically dangerous story, she claims, because according to tradition a woman names Jesus with her prophetic sign-action.[5] What implications does the story of this woman have for women's apostolic and ministerial leadership in the Christian community?

4. How can you continue the ministry of the woman who anoints Jesus in your life and in our world today?

PRAYER EXPERIENCE

1. Take some deep breaths…. Find a comfortable position…. As you inhale, count slowly to five…. As you exhale, count slowly to five…. Do this for several minutes or until you feel calm and centered….

2. Read the scripture slowly…. Imagine that you are present as this scene unfolds…. Visualize the woman entering the house of Simon the leper…with an alabaster jar full of very costly ointment…. Observe her break open the jar…. The noise resounds through the room…. Watch her as she anoints the head of Jesus…confidently…lovingly…. Smell the fragrant perfume that fills the room…. Look at Jesus…. Reflect for a moment on how Jesus feels…. Reflect on the courage…and deep love of the woman as the anointing takes place…. She gives all…empties her perfume…risks everything, including her social standing…by her daring act of anointing Jesus…naming Jesus…as the Christ, the Messiah…. Listen to the angry complaints of the male disciples…. "Why was the ointment wasted this way?"… Reflect on their resistance to the woman's actions…. Now listen to Jesus' defense and affirmation of the woman's prophetic action…. "Let her alone, why do you trouble her?… She has performed a good service for me…. She has done what she could; she has anointed my body for its burial…. Truly I tell you, wherever the good news is proclaimed in the whole world, what she has done will be told in remembrance of her."…

3. Claim this promise of Jesus for this woman in some life-giving way…. Do something in remembrance of her today….

4. Ponder the image of the costly ointment.... Spend time with this symbol, and let it speak to you of extravagant love.... Imagine your love as costly ointment.... Who will you pour it out on?... Will you give it all?... How will you anoint Christ in your life?...in our world?... Are you willing to break through societal norms and deal with hostility ...rejection...anger...from those who don't understand?... Who and what will give you strength to risk everything for so great a love?...

5. Dialogue with the woman who anoints Jesus about the implications that her actions have had on women's apostolic and ministerial leadership in the Christian community today.... Use perfumed oil and anoint yourself and/or others for service, leadership, or some specific ministry to the community.... As you do so, play some soft, instrumental music in the background....

6. Compose a litany, prayer, poem, song, dance, ritual to celebrate your anointing...and/or to celebrate contemporary women as disciples and Christian witnesses....

7. In your prayer journal, note any thoughts, feelings, insights, images, or sensations generated by this reflection.... Plan to share, if possible, your reflections with others in a sacred circle.

Mary, Mother of Jesus

⟋⟍

The Bible portrays Mary as the Mother of Jesus and the wife of Joseph who conceived her baby through the power of the Holy Spirit while she was a virgin. The story of the virgin birth is told in two different places in scripture. Matthew's Gospel presents the story from the point of view of Joseph. The angel appears before Joseph and tells him, "Do not be afraid to take Mary as your wife, for the child conceived in her is from the Holy Spirit. She will bear a son, and you are to name him Jesus, for he will save his people from their sins" (Mt 1:20–21). Luke tells the story from the perspective of Mary. In Luke, the angel appears to Mary saying, "Do not be afraid, Mary, for you have found favor with God. And now, you will conceive in your womb and bear a son, and you will name him Jesus" (Lk 1:30–31). Mary asks the angel to explain how this will happen since she is a virgin. Then the angel responds: "The Holy Spirit will come upon you, and the power of the Most High will overshadow you; therefore the child to be born will be holy; he will be called Son of God" (Lk 1:35). The accounts of the conception of Jesus in Matthew and Luke are similar. Matthew says that Mary's child will be conceived through the Holy Spirit, while Luke says he will be conceived through the power of the Most High. Then Mary went to visit her cousin, Elizabeth, who was already six months pregnant. "When Elizabeth heard Mary's greeting, her baby leaped in her womb. She welcomed Mary with great joy, 'Blessed are you among women, and

blessed is the fruit of your womb. And why has this happened
to me, that the mother of my Lord comes to me?'" (Lk 1:41–
43). Then Mary proclaims her famous hymn of jubilant praise,
which has become known as the Magnificat. This prayer
emphasizes God's power and mercy for the lowly and oppressed. Mary remained with Elizabeth for three months and
then returned to Joseph. The second chapter of Luke and the
first chapter of Matthew recount one of the most popular
and beautiful stories in Christianity—the birth of Jesus (Lk
2;1–20; Mt 1:18–25). After the birth of Jesus, the family fled
to Egypt to avoid Herod's persecution. Then they returned to
their home in Nazareth where the child grew in strength and
wisdom. scripture does not give us a lot of details about their
family life. Luke recounts the circumcision, presentation of
Jesus in the Temple, and the story of the twelve-year-old Jesus
in the Temple (Lk 2:21–52). How did Mary respond to these
events? Luke provides a clue: "His mother treasured all these
things in her heart" (Lk 2:51).[1]

When Jesus begins his public ministry, Mary shows up on
several important occasions. She is with Jesus at the Wedding Feast of Cana. Noticing that the wine supply is dwin-
dling, Mary tells Jesus: "They have no wine" (Jn 2:3). Jesus
responds to his mother's concern that the wedding family be
spared embarrassment by changing water into wine, a miracle
he clearly never intended. She hastens thereby the public
announcement of his prophetic ministry and demonstrates
her leadership role in the community. This was, as the gospel
points out, "the first of his signs, in Cana of Galilee, and revealed his glory; and his disciples believed in him" (Jn 2:11).
The Synoptics provide another glimpse of Mary when she
appears one day with Jesus' brothers and sisters. On that oc-
casion Jesus proclaims that Christian discipleship broadens
family bonds. "Whoever does the will of God is my brother
and sister and mother." In other words, for those who live a

faith life within the believing community, the bonds of spiritual kinship supersede family ties (Mk 3:31–35; Mt 12:46–50; Lk 8:19–21). But Jesus does not negate his own family tie to Mary. She, above all others, shows herself to be one who "does the will of God." Mary is with Jesus in his greatest hour of suffering on the cross. "When Jesus saw his mother and the disciple whom he loved standing beside her, he said to his mother, 'Woman, here is your son.' Then he said to the disciple, 'Here is your mother.' And from that hour the disciple took her into his home" (Jn 19:26–27). The last mention of Mary is when she was gathered with the disciples in the upper room in Jerusalem. "All these were constantly devoting themselves to prayer, together with certain women, including Mary the mother of Jesus, as well as his brothers" (Acts 1:14). Here is Mary with the very men who left her son in his time of greatest need, with one who had served as a leader, but who, when push came to shove, actually denied knowing her son. Here she is with a bunch of cowards (except for John), who were too fearful for their own necks to stand beside her at the cross watching Jesus' gruesome public execution! When she needed their support, they were not there for her. But in the upper room she is not blaming; she is not condemning; rather she is there with them in the prayer-room, supporting them by her presence when they are feeling most guilty, most blemished, most unredeemable, most forlorn. She is supporting those who have just failed to support her and Jesus! Does that not suggest an amazing depth of insight and compassion? Here Mary's compassion is commensurate with that of Jesus who kept on saying, as they crucified him: "Abba, forgive them because *they don't know what they are doing!*" (Lk 23:34, *The Inclusive New Testament*).

Throughout the ages, devotion to Mary has been characteristic of the Catholic tradition. As early as the third century, there are drawings of Mary holding the Christ child in the catacombs of Domitilla in Rome. Justin, the martyr, refers to Mary in his writings as the "new Eve." Some theologians believe that Mariology (devotion to Mary) must be understood in the context of the tremendous need of Christians down the centuries for the "mothering" side of our God who was most often depicted in terms of King, triumphant Lord, Warrior Prince, Great Ruler, and Judge. This distancing of God worsened during the centuries of the Arian heresy, because the divinity of Jesus was overemphasized to counteract the effects of the heresy. Ordinary people were made to feel too sinful and unworthy to approach the divine Jesus, let alone the Godhead. This distancing of the human person from God was reemphasized in church architecture that placed the action of the liturgy behind walls, restricted to a male clergy alone. The job of the laity, laymen and women, on their side of the screen, was to worship in obscurity and pray with humility. God was one before whom we could merely beat our breasts and hope for mercy. In this cold, masculine, religious sphere, the one gentle, redeeming, human person was Mary. Some scholars refer to the unwillingness of early Mediterranean Christianity to let go of the feminine element in religion. Rather, it seems that the human psyche is hungry for the total reality of a God who so cares for us as to create human beings as the pinnacle of God's birthing of the world. We sustain a natural, psychological, and spiritual need for feminine metaphors that depict such a nurturing, comforting God. Mary was the ever-present, perfect metaphor—although not divine herself—of the mothering aspect of divinity that human beings craved. In today's Christian understanding she remains the most perfect icon or image by which we can understand the mothering side of God.

Contemporary theologians are constructing a new liberating portrait of Mary today which relates to the real life issues of women and which challenges those assumptions that stereotype women as passive and submissive. Anne Carr reflects on the potential of this new consciousness to provide a more integrated understanding of Mary for our times:

> Mary as virgin and mother need not be understood as an impossible double bind, an inimitable ideal, but as a central Christian symbol that signifies autonomy and relationship, strength and tenderness, struggle and victory, God's power and human agency—not in competition, but in cooperation.[2]

One of the great treasures that can help us contemplate Mary in fresh ways is her prayer of praise, the Magnificat. This song of joy proclaimed by Mary when she met Elizabeth resembles the Song of Hannah, the mother of Samuel (1 Sm 2:1–10). In both prayers, emphasis is on praising God for lifting up the lowly and nourishing the hungry. Women are still the lowliest in many modern societies. There is a sense of women's solidarity with the lowliest and hungriest, expressed by putting these two songs in the mouths of women.[3]

In our Catholic tradition no one who is in God's eternal present is far from us. We experience a connectedness and friendship with Mary and the saints who have preceded us. In praying the Magnificat, we stand with Mary, the simple, teenaged, pregnant but unmarried woman of faith, in her clairvoyant perception of God's relationship with us, through the strong language of her prayer. In this prayer, Mary is a symbol of strength, comfort, and power for the disinherited and powerless of the world. She is companion, champion, and change-agent for the righteous poor, who will triumph over oppression and experience the justice promised to them by God. Today more than ever we need to discover a larger vision of the liberating power of Mary's woman-spirit in our midst. As we reclaim Mary as our sister and friend, we will find much in her life that relates to our own hopes, dreams, and struggles, and much that points us to a Mothering God.

MARY'S SONG OF PRAISE/MAGNIFICAT

"Mary said:
'My soul proclaims your greatness, O God,
and my spirit rejoices in you, my Savior,
for you have looked with favor
upon your lowly servant,
and from this day forward
all generations will call me blessed.
For you, the Almighty, have done great things for me,
and holy is your Name.
Your mercy reaches from age to age
for those who fear you.
You have shown strength with your arm,
you have scattered the proud in their conceit,
you have deposed the mighty from their thrones
and raised the lowly to high places.
You have filled the hungry with good things,
while you have sent the rich away empty.
You have come to the aid of Israel your servant,
mindful of your mercy—
the promise you made to our ancestors—
to Sarah and Abraham
and their descendants forever'"
(Lk 1:46–55, *The Inclusive New Testament*).

DISCUSSION STARTERS

1. Reflect on traditional Catholic devotions to Mary. What impact do these devotional practices have on people's faith?

2. How do you experience Mary as a companion, champion, and change-agent? How has Mary influenced your spirituality?

3. Reflect on the Magnificat. How is Mary, a poor person, a symbol of strength, comfort, and power for the disinherited and powerless of the world?

4. Do you agree that Mary gave Catholics an opportunity to experience the divine reality in the person of a woman?

PRAYER EXPERIENCE

1. Be aware of tension in your body. Release the tension by breathing relaxation into this area of your body. As you inhale, breathe in your Mothering God's liberating power. As you exhale, allow this freeing power of God's nurturing love to flow out of you and fill the oppressed people of the world with justice and peace.

2. A variety of names and images have been used to describe Mary, such as "First Disciple," "Mother of the Church," "Ark of the Covenant," "Model of Openness," "Queen of Peace," "Comforter of the Afflicted," "Cause of our Joy," "Liberator of the Oppressed," "Mystical Rose," and so on. Compose a litany using some of your favorite names or images for Mary. You may select one of these names or images, or create your own, and use it as a mantra or short prayer that you can repeat during times of prayer.

3. Reflect on Mary's Song of Praise/the Magnificat. Choose one image or concept from this prayer for contemplation. Allow it to sink into the depths of your being. Simply be present in deep love and openness.

4. Invite Mary, a poor person, a symbol of strength, comfort, and power for the disinherited to preach a sermon today to the powerful leaders and institutions that oppress and dominate the powerless of the world. What would this champion of human rights say? How would the powerful respond to her? Invite Mary to be a change-agent for the oppressed of the world. What would this change-agent do for the oppressed? How would they respond? Reflect on ways that you can be a champion and change-agent in the lives of the oppressed people in your family, neighborhood, city, and world.

5. Pray for the needs of your sisters and brothers, the hungriest, poorest and lowliest, who have not yet learned to cry out for themselves. Cry out to *Shaddai** for them. Decide on one step you can take to help them experience liberation and empowerment in their lives.

6. Reflect on Mary as sister and friend. Experience the liberating power of Mary's woman-spirit touching your life. Share your heart's longings, hopes, dreams, and struggles with her. Invite her to share her story with you.

7. Find or create a symbol of your relationship with Mary and put it in a prominent place in your home. Reflect on any wisdom, strength, courage, faith, compassion, love, etc. that came to you during this time of prayer. Record your feelings, images, thoughts, insights, decisions in a journal, poetry, art, song, dance, or in some other creative way.

---

*A name for God found in the Hebrew scripture that can be translated, "God, the breasted one."

JUNIA

❧

I n Romans 16:7, Paul identifies Junia and Andronicus as
"outstanding apostles." It is the only time that Paul refers
to someone other than the Twelve or himself as apostles. Some
biblical translators changed Junia, a female name, to the male
name Junias, and up until recent years the male name appeared in most Bibles. However, tradition does not support
this name change. Junia was a common female name in the
Roman Empire at the time of the early Christian missionary
movement. Patristic sources acknowledged Junia as an apostle.
The fourth-century bishop of Constantinople, John
Chrysostom, recognized Junia as a member of the apostolic
circle: "Oh, how great is the devotion of this woman that she
should be counted worthy of the appellation of apostle!"[1] In
addition, several other well-known scholars such as Origen
of Alexandria, Saint Jerome, Hatto of Vercelli, Theophylact,
and Peter Abelard agreed that Junia was a woman apostle. In
fact, the first commentator on this text who changed her name
to the masculine form Junias was Aegidus of Rome (1245–
1316). Unfortunately, this action removed this outstanding
woman apostle from biblical texts until recent scholarship
rediscovered her.[2]

Commenting on the contortions that resulted in a sex
change by translation, Elizabeth A. Castelli notes:

> The feminine name Junia is replaced in modern trans-
> lations by the masculine name Junias, a name nowhere

else attested in the ancient world. Once again the argument is a circular syllogism: since, by definition, women
cannot be apostles, when a woman is called an apostle,
she is either not an apostle or she is not a woman.[3]

Some scholars believe that Andronicus was the husband
of Junia and both shared a partnership in ministry like that
of Prisca and Aquila and other missionary couples in the early
Church. In 1 Corinthians 9:5, Paul argues that he, like the
other apostles, was accompanied on his missionary missions
by female partners. Hence, couple ministry appears to have
been the trend in the beginning of the Christian movement.
However, it is important to point out that neither Junia nor
Prisca are referred to as wives. What seems to be significant
is not their status as wives but rather their commitment as
coworkers and partners in preaching the gospel. Ross Saunders
believes that this is important because "it shows that Paul
accepted her on her own right and not just as the wife of
Andronicus."[4] In addition, there is no evidence that the ministry of these women missionaries was limited to women, as
some patristic sources imply.[5]

More than likely, Junia and Andronicus had become Christians before Paul, had been coworkers with Paul in Antioch,
and had been persecuted and suffered imprisonment with Paul
for the Christian faith: "Greet Andronicus and Junia, my relatives who were in prison with me; they are prominent among
the apostles, and they were in Christ before I was" (Rom 16:7).
It is possible that they were members of the apostolic circle
in Jerusalem who, together with James, experienced a vision
of the Risen Christ (see 1 Cor 15:7).[6]

So what is the significance of Junia, outstanding woman
apostle, today? She was invisible to us for centuries. What do
you suppose would surprise her about women's roles and status in the Church today? If she could preach a sermon to the

world on women's roles and status what would she say? What if she were to join women and men of all ages, races, religions, cultures, and nations who are speaking out for justice; standing up for truth; advocating systemic change of oppressive societal structures; speaking out against power-hungry leaders who create wars and human devastation for their own avaricious ends; networking for the poor, oppressed, and disadvantaged; promoting human rights, equal rights, and minority rights; and insisting on monetary, political, healthcare, educational, welfare, and prison reform? How would her experience as apostle relate to contemporary women's and men's experiences of gospel commitment? Perhaps Junia, companion, champion, and change-agent might provide us with some new insights, interesting perspectives, and exciting challenges on these tough questions.

REFLECTION

"Greet Andronicus and Junia, my relatives who were in prison with me; they are prominent among the apostles, and they were in Christ before I was" (Rom 16:7).

DISCUSSION STARTERS

1. Do you think Junia was a woman apostle equal to Paul, Andronicus, and the Twelve? Why? Why not?
2. Why is it important to reclaim Junia as a woman apostle today? Can you name some contemporary women apostles? Are you one?
3. If you could ask Junia a question(s), what would it be? If Junia could ask women and men in the contemporary Church a question(s), what would it be?

4. Do you think Jesus called women to be apostles? Do you think Jesus calls women to apostolic leadership in the Church today?

   Why? Why not?

Prayer Experience

1. Be aware of your breathing.... Surround yourself with quiet and peace. Use a prayer phrase, or mantra, to help you relax and be still.... Holy One of Courage, fill me.... Holy One of Justice, fill me.... Holy One of Peace, fill me.... Holy One of Liberation, fill me.... Holy One of Compassion, fill me...and so on.

2. Imagine that you are Junia.... You and Andronicus have just finished up an exhausting missionary journey... preaching...teaching...healing...delivering people from bondage...celebrating the joyful love of your Christian life.... Now both of you have been put in prison.... Paul is there, too.... The three of you suffer humiliation... harassment...and other deprivations.... You share your sufferings and support one another...praying...singing hymns of praise...strengthening...encouraging...comforting...and challenging one another.... You feel Christ's presence in one another.... The power of the Holy Spirit is upon you.... There is something important you want to say to Andronicus and Paul.... Now is the time to do so....

3. Be aware of ways that you have suffered for the gospel.... Reflect on times that you have suffered in some way(s) for your faith...values...ideals...beliefs...etc.... Offer thanks for the people who strengthened you...encouraged you...uplifted you...challenged you...empowered you....

4. Reflect on your life as a Christian... Did you ever endanger your life for the gospel?... Did you ever risk your repu-

tation for truth?…justice?…peace? Do you love others generously?… Do you have compassion for the sufferings of others, especially the poor and needy?… If you were arrested tomorrow for being a Christian, would there be enough evidence to convict you?… Write down your answers to these questions…. Ask forgiveness for any failures you are aware of…. Give thanks for ways that you have been able to take risks for the gospel….

5. Be aware of opportunities you have to join women and men of all ages, races, religions, cultures, and nations who are speaking out for justice…standing up for truth… advocating systemic change of oppressive societal structures…networking for the poor, oppressed, and disadvantaged…promoting human rights, equal rights, and minority rights…and insisting on monetary, political, health-care, educational, welfare, and prison reform…. Decide on one way you can join with others to take action on behalf of justice in our world…. Pray for all people who witness the gospel throughout the world in courageous ways….

6. Dialogue with Junia about her experience(s) as apostle. Share your experience(s) of gospel commitment with her. … Are there any questions that you would like to ask her? … Allow these questions to become prayers arising from the depths of your being…. Are there any questions that Junia would like to ask you?… Allow these questions, also, to become prayers arising from the depths of your being….

7. Reflect on ways that you can be like the apostle Junia; a leader in the contemporary Church…. Pray for a new outpouring of the Spirit in our time: for example,

> O Fire of Pentecost,
> come and pour out the fullness of your gifts on
> us today,

Like our sister, the apostle Junia,
may we be filled with your Holy Spirit
and dance in the new creation
as radiant witnesses of your glorious presence
everywhere we go.
May your Church empower us to preach the
gospel and stand up for justice for ourselves and
others everyday of our lives.
AMEN.

Record, if you wish, any thoughts...feelings...or insights from this prayer experience in a prayer journal, poetry, art, dance, or in some other creative way.

PHOEBE

❦

I n Romans, Paul commends deacon Phoebe of the church
at Cenchreae near Corinth, as a leader and missionary. He
exhorts the community to welcome her and "help her in whatever she may require from you, for she has been a benefactor
of many and of myself as well" (Rom 16:2). It is interesting to
observe that Paul identifies Phoebe as *diakonos*, which means
deacon. Paul's reference to Phoebe as "our sister and *diakonos*"
is the same word used to describe Timothy as "our brother
and God's *diakonos*" (1 Thes 3:2) and Tychicus as "our beloved brother and faithful *diakonoss*" (Col 4:7). In the past,
this term was translated "missionary" or "minister" when applied to men, but as "helper" or "deaconess" when referred to
Phoebe. Also, Paul calls Phoebe a "leader," *prostatis*, not a
"helper" as the term is usually translated. This word appears
nowhere else in the Christian scriptures and always means
leader or overseer. It is obvious that Paul acknowledges
Phoebe's influential position as leader in the early Christian
missionary movement. She is first on Paul's greeting list in
his letter to the Romans. Paul expects the Christian community in Rome to treat this woman missionary and teacher
with the hospitality and support that her ministry deserves.
He exhorts them to "welcome her…as is fitting for the saints
…and help her in whatever she may require from you…" (Rom
16:2). Scholars today believe that Phoebe was entrusted with
the mission to proclaim Paul's letter to the house churches in

Rome, since they know from research that such carefully worded documents were not only carried by the messenger, but proclaimed rhetorically. They also conclude that Phoebe was an influential leader whose authority and credentials were accepted by the local church.[1]

As a servant of God and a person with authority in the community, Phoebe devoted herself to the mission of Jesus. Paul refers to her as a benefactor of many people, including himself. She was a businesswoman in Cenchreae, evidently successful enough to become a financier of several missionary ventures. Her patronage assured Paul of financial support, hospitality, and prestigious connections. According to the law of Greco-Roman patronage, Paul invites the Christian community of Rome to repay Phoebe for the assistance and support Paul owes her as client. This seems to suggest that Phoebe was a well-educated, rich woman of independent means. Paul's letter implies that not only did Phoebe use her resources and wealth to help him, but she also assisted people who were suffering, poor, and oppressed. It seems evident from his commendation that Phoebe's preaching, teaching, and ministry made a powerful impact on Paul and on the first-century church of Rome.[2]

Contemporary scholars observe that women leaders like Phoebe were not assistants to the apostles, but rather were apostles, missionaries, and leaders of communities equal to and independent of Paul. They did not receive their authority from Paul, nor owe their positions to him. Rather, it is probable that Paul cooperated with these women and recognized their authority within the communities.[3]

Phoebe's story challenges women in ministry to be biblical scholars. Romans was written by Paul, but Phoebe proclaimed it. As Carolyn D. Baker said it: "Paul wrote the doctrines. Phoebe explained them. No Phoebe, no Romans.... The Church needs women with Bible-rich blood."[4]

Phoebe is a model for women in ministry today. As an independent, confident, and generous woman, she shared her abundant resources with others. She was aware of her spiritual power and authority. She was willing to take the daring risk of travel to Rome in an era when all travel was difficult and dangerous. She lived her call to the fullest. In her teaching, preaching, and ministry, Phoebe witnessed to the gospel and contributed to the growth of the Church. Like Phoebe, contemporary women are called to be official teachers and leaders in the Church. The Christian community today needs women in ministry more than ever. As Paul trusted Phoebe to proclaim the gospel, so now the Church needs to recognize women as influential leaders in the believing community. One way this is happening is through the grass-roots development of contemporary house churches and sacred circles.

REFLECTION

"I commend to you our sister Phoebe, a deacon of the church at Cenchreae, so that you may welcome her in [God] as is fitting for the saints, and help her in whatever she may require from you, for she has been a benefactor of many and of myself as well" (Rom 16:1–2).

DISCUSSION STARTERS

1. Phoebe was independent, confident, and generous. She was aware of her spiritual power and authority. She lived her call to the fullest. Comment on these characteristics and how they impact on Christian ministry.
2. In what way(s) is Phoebe a model for women in ministry today?

3. How did Phoebe and Paul exhibit a partnership in the gospel?

4. What impact do women who preach, teach, and minister have on the mission of Jesus Christ today?

Prayer Experience

1. Relax for a few minutes in silence. Breathe slowly and deeply. As you inhale, be conscious of God's boundless love surrounding you…filling you…empowering you. As you exhale, breathe out God's love for yourself…family …friends…coworkers…neighbors…all people…all creation.

2. Contemplate yourself as a reflection of God's passionate love for family…friends…coworkers…neighbors…all people…all creation….

3. Reflect on Phoebe's ministry in the early Church…. Invite her to minister to you as a sister, and partner, in the gospel…. Gather with her in a sacred circle of women or in a contemporary house church….

4. Create an image, phrase, prayer, song, dance, art piece that expresses your understanding of God's call in your life…. Put it in a prominent place as a special reminder of God's love active in you…touching…liberating…healing …empowering…others….

5. Reflect on the leadership gifts that you share with others in your ministry…and that others share with you in their ministry to you…. Make a list of them…. Offer a prayer of thanks for these gifts….

6. Be aware of any new possibilities or challenges that are present in your ministry…. Ask God to help you to lead in ways that will be life-giving for you and for others….

7. Create a ritual or prayer that you can use to celebrate your

commitment to witness...preach...teach...live the gospel.... If possible, share it with others to whom...for whom...and with whom...you minister...in a quiet moment or in a festive celebration....

PRISCA (PRISCILLA)

෴

When Claudius expelled the Jews from Rome, Prisca (or Priscilla) and her husband Aquila moved to Corinth where they joined Paul in his work and ministry. Like Paul, they were Jewish Christians and tentmakers. Like Barnabas, Prisca and Aquila were missionaries and coworkers with Paul. Their house churches in Corinth, Ephesus, and Rome were centers of missionary activity and Christian life.

Prisca is mentioned six times in the Christian scriptures. Though Prisca and Aquila worked together as a ministry team, in four out of six places her name is mentioned first. This indicates that she is the more prominent of the two in the first-century Church.[1]

The Church gathered in their home, in Rome (Rom 16:3–5), and in Corinth and Ephesus (Acts 18:18; 2 Tm 4:19; 1 Cor 16:19). Prisca, in addition to being a coworker of Paul and a partner in ministry with Aquila, is a missionary apostle, a teacher of a missionary apostle, and an important leader in the development of house churches.

Romans 16 uses the word *eklesia*—"church"—to describe the group gathered in their home: "Greet Prisca and Aquila, who work with me in Christ Jesus, and who risked their necks for my life, to whom not only I give thanks, but also all the churches of the Gentiles. Greet also the church in their house" (Rom 16:3–5). This text reflects the courage of these missionary coworkers of Paul who were willing to endanger their lives because of their love for him.

When Paul left Corinth for Syria, Prisca and Aquila accompanied him on a missionary journey to Ephesus where he left them (Acts 18:18–19). There Prisca and Aquila encountered Apollos, an eloquent and learned missionary. After hearing him speak in the synagogue, they realized he had only a superficial knowledge of the Christian faith and needed further instructions in the Way of God. So they became his teachers (Acts 18:24–28). "Prisca, in particular," observes Elisabeth Schussler Fiorenza, "became the teacher of Apollos, whose Sophia and Spirit theology might have been derived from her catechesis."[2] John Chrysostom attributes to her "the whole merit of having instructed Apollos correctly in Christian Doctrine."[3]

When Paul returned, about a year later, he discovered that this couple had developed an effective, strong community in Ephesus. Later, Paul, in his first letter to the Corinthians from Ephesus, included their salutations: "Aquila and Prisca together with the church in their house, greet you warmly..." (1 Cor 16:19). In his exhortation to Timothy before his approaching death, Paul sends final greetings to Prisca and Aquila: "Greet Prisca and Aquila..." (2 Tm 4:19).[4]

Historical records, not found in the Bible, describe Priscilla's renown. Tertullian writes, "By the holy Prisca, the Gospel is preached." *Coemeterium Priscilla*, one of the ancient Roman catacombs, was named after her. A Roman church, "Titulus St. Prisca," was built in her honor and her name was inscribed on monuments in Rome.[5]

There is much that contemporary Christians can learn from Prisca and Aquila about team ministry, preaching, eucharistic sharing, and community building. This couple ministry team traveled together and created house churches for converts. Prisca and Aquila modeled partnership in the gospel and a vision of caring community that is as important in our times as it was in their era. They did not, like Paul, separate the proclamation of the Word that focuses on conversion from the eucharistic table-sharing that builds community.[6]

One of the positive signs of our times is that the Church is rediscovering the importance of vibrant Christian communities for faith-sharing and spiritual life. The difficulty, however, is that for many people, the Word and Eucharist have become separated because of the shortage of ordained priests. What seems to be needed is a whole new theology of ministry in the Church. Prisca and Aquila provide a female/male partnership ministry model that can inspire and challenge us. Likewise, we need creative reflection and serious discussion on the effectiveness of our female/male experience of team ministry today, as well as a deeper understanding of Eucharist as the Christ presence in our midst.

REFLECTION

"After this Paul left Athens and went to Corinth. There he found a Jew named Aquila, a native of Pontus, who had recently come from Italy with his wife Priscilla, because Claudius had ordered all Jews to leave Rome. Paul went to see them, and, because he was of the same trade, he stayed with them, and they worked together—by trade they were tentmakers" (Acts 18:1–3).

"The churches of Asia send greetings. Aquila and Prisca, together with the church in their house, greet you warmly in the Lord" (1 Cor 16:19).

"Greet Prisca and Aquila who work with me in Christ Jesus, and who risked their necks for my life, to whom not only I give thanks, but also all the churches of the Gentiles" (Rom 16:3–4).

"Greet Prisca and Aquila and the household of Onesiphorus" (2 Tm 4:19).

DISCUSSION STARTERS

1. Prisca and Aquila provide a model of female/male partnership in ministry. How do you think their ministry
   helped them to grow in their relationship with one another? How do you think their relationship with one another helped them to grow in their ministry?
2. In what ways is female/male partnership in ministry effective today?
3. Compare and contrast the house churches of first-century
   Christianity with the Small Christian Community Movement in our Church today. What are the similarities? What
   are the differences?
4. Have you ever been a member of a Small Christian Community (such as "Renew," "Gather," Charismatic prayer
   group, Bible study group, faith-sharing group, Woman
   Church, Marriage Encounter, Cursillo, and the like)? If
   so, describe your experiences. If not, describe the kind of
   community that would appeal to you.

PRAYER EXPERIENCE

1. Quiet your mind and your body.... Take several deep
   breaths.... With your eyes closed and your body relaxed,
   journey to your still point where God dwells.... Be still in
   God's presence.
2. Read the scripture texts about Prisca and Aquila slowly
   and thoughtfully.
3. Imagine Prisca and Aquila as a loving couple...affectionate
   with one another...passionate about the gospel...willing
   to travel anywhere with missionary zeal to share the Good
   News...desiring to do anything...risking everything to
   proclaim Christ...nurturing community in their house

church...committing all their energy to the Christian mission....

4. Be aware of times in your life when you experienced female/ male partnership in ministry.... Be conscious of the advantages you experienced...and disadvantages you experienced.... Be conscious of ways your female/male team ministry helped you to grow...helped your partner to grow. ... Be conscious of ways this partnership ministered to the needs of others...enriched the Christian community....

5. Draw an image or symbol of this partnership in ministry.... Hang it in a prominent place in your place of ministry.... Perhaps you may wish to share your reflections and this symbol or image with your partner....

6. Reflect on your vision of female/male partnership in ministry in the Church today.... Get in touch with your feelings...hopes...frustrations...dreams...challenges....

7. Write down your vision...images...insights...thoughts... feelings...in a journal, poetry, art, song, dance, or in some other creative way.

LYDIA

❧

Lydia, an influential and successful businesswoman of Philippi, was a "seller of purple goods." These luxury items may have been either a secretion of a species of mollusk or murex or purple-dyed cloths. More than likely, she was self-supporting and financially independent. There is no mention of male relatives. She was the head of her household. Perhaps she dressed often in purple as she walked through the streets of Philippi. There, by the banks of the Gangites River, she met with a circle of Jewish women to worship God, although she probably was not Jewish. The term "worshiper of God" referred to a Gentile who attended Jewish services and believed in Jewish teachings about God. Here at a Sabbath service, Paul and Silas met with the women and related the Gospel of Jesus Christ. As Lydia heard the message, God opened her heart "to listen eagerly to what was said by Paul." Soon afterward she and her household were baptized. The text does not reveal whether those who were baptized were family members or business associates. In either case, they followed Lydia's lead. After her baptism Lydia provided hospitality to Paul and Silas in her home (Acts 16:14–15).[1]

Then, Lydia, the first Christian convert in Europe, began the church of Philippi. A group of Christians gathered in her home. This "house church" became a popular meeting place for eucharistic liturgies and provided safe haven for persecuted Christians. After Paul's release from prison, for freeing a female slave from demon possession, Paul and Silas went immediately to Lydia's house and "encouraged the brothers and sisters there" (Acts 16:40). Paul's letter to the Philippians showed his deep affection for this community. "I thank my God every time I remember you, constantly praying with joy in every one of my prayers for all of you, because of your sharing in the gospel from the first day until now" (Phil 1:3–5).

Lydia, like Priscilla and Phoebe, was an initiator and leading figure in the local church. She was a partner with Paul and Silas in spreading the gospel. Her house church was a center of missionary activity. Members included families, relatives, converts, former slaves, and clients and looked more like a religious association than a patriarchal family. They were a new people, women and men equals, working side by side in the spreading of the gospel.[2] Lydia, our biblical sister, reminds us that partnership in the Church is not only possible and important, but is a constitutive dimension of proclaiming the gospel in our times.

These women used their spiritual power and authority as servant leaders of house churches to gather Christians together for the breaking of the bread and table-sharing. The head of the household usually presided over the breaking of bread. Although the Christian scripture does not reveal who, among the early Christians, presided over these meals, one can assume that it was the household leader. Therefore, it is probable that these women functioned in a role that later would be identified as presbyter, or priest. As household heads, these women reflected on scripture, sang songs of praise, broke the bread, blessed the cup, and shared it with their guests in a communal meal.

Scholars today are taking a new look at the important roles women played in the early Church. Women in Philippi were attracted to Paul's preaching of a gospel in which men and women were of equal value.[3] Some believe that women functioned as priests and bishops. One such expert, Dr. Dorothy

Irvin, a theologian and photographer for the Biblical Ar-
chaeological Institute of Tubingen, has collected mosaics,
inscriptions, and other pictorial depictions including "a fresco,
dating to the end of the first century, in a Roman catacomb,
which depicts a group of seven women celebrating a Eucharist"—all of which provide evidence for this claim.[4]

Lydia was a convert energized by the Spirit ("Christ opened
her heart"), and exuded the kind of spiritual energy that welcomed people around the eucharistic table in her home. As
Mary Lou Sleevi says in her poetic painting of Lydia:

> Church in Philippi
> sprang from a base—
> from a family, or two,
> formed by the Word.
> Paul longed to come back.
> His letter to the Philippians,
> written in prison,
> may have been read the first time
> to a church gathered for supper
> at Lydia's house....
> To Philippi was given
> the Epistle of Joy.[5]

REFLECTION

"We set sail from Troas and took a straight course to
Samothrace, the following day to Neapolis, and from there
to Philippi, which is a leading city of the district of Macedonia
and a Roman colony. We remained in this city for some days.
On the Sabbath day we went outside the gate by the river,
where we supposed there was a place of prayer, and we sat
down and spoke to the women who had gathered there. A

certain woman named Lydia, a worshiper of God, was listening to us; she from the city of Thyatira and a dealer in purple cloth. [God] opened her heart to listen eagerly to what was said by Paul. When she and her household were baptized, she urged us, saying, 'If you have judged me to be faithful to God, come and stay at my home.' And she prevailed upon us" (Acts 16:11–15).

"After leaving prison they went to Lydia's home; and when they had seen and encouraged the brothers and sisters there, they departed" (Acts 16:40).

DISCUSSION STARTERS

1. Lydia was a leader, initiator, and presider at table-sharing in the house church in Philippi. How is she a mentor for women in ministry in the contemporary Church?

2. Consider the issue of women's ordination. In light of recent findings, do you think women were ordained in the early Christian tradition? Why? Why not?

3. What are your thoughts and feelings on the issues relating to women's ordination in the contemporary Church? What is your reaction to the Vatican's recent ban on discussion of this topic?

4. How can women and men work together in a partnership of equals to transform sexism and patriarchy in our society and Church? Give examples.

PRAYER EXPERIENCE

1. Select some classical or instrumental music to accompany your reflection…. Begin by playing the piece you select. Surround yourself with calm and tranquillity….

2. You are invited to attend a meal…. Before you come to the table you bring a special gift with you to nourish another's joy…hope…love….

3. You are now entering the room…. There is a round table …comfortable chairs around the table…. There are beautiful flowers…. Several candles are lit on brass stands around the room…. The table is set with the most beautiful dishes…glassware…silver setting…you have ever seen…. You smell home-baked bread and cakes…. There seems to be an abundance of delicious drinks…sparkling water, wine, tea, coffee…. There are fruits…vegetables…and some of your favorite foods…. Some special people are there…family members…friends…community members…strangers…church officials…feminist theologians…women and men from your local church community…people you have never met before…. All of you are seated around the table….

4. Your hostess opens the banquet with a prayer…. Then during the meal she invites guests to share their special gifts with the group…. As they do so, there is lots of laughter and a few tears…. You share prayers, stories, songs…. You break bread and share the cup…. You give thanks…. You share something very special…. People respond to your gift…. You become aware of your thoughts…images…feelings…insights…. You have a deeper understanding of the others gathered around the table with you….

5. Your hostess dramatizes a contemporary version of Lydia's story that addresses sexism and patriarchy in Church and society today….

   As she speaks of her experiences…the room is quiet…. You are amazed by what she says and does…. You have some questions…concerns…you would like to ask her…. You have some questions…concerns you would like to express about the contemporary Church's attitude toward women in ministry in the Church…. You notice others in the group want to respond also….

6. The group takes several minutes for private reflection on "Contemporary Lydias."… Then the group shares in small and large groups…. You find this an exciting…frustrating …powerful…challenging…experience.

7. The group decides to do something that will help change sexist and patriarchal attitudes toward women in Church and society….

    They plan to invite the following people_____ and groups_____ to join them.

MARY,
MOTHER OF JOHN MARK

⚉

M ary, mother of John Mark, was a leader of one of the house churches in Jerusalem. Scholars believe that Hellenist or Greek Christians—not the Hebrew Christians associated with James—gathered in her home. She was an independent woman with considerable resources, including a spacious home which became an important center for first-century Christians to meet for worship and prayer. Some commentators believe that Mary presided at Eucharist there and that her home was the headquarters of the Jerusalem church.[1] It is significant that this "Mary" did not sell her house and give the proceeds to the apostles for the common need as described in Acts; and that she dedicated her home as a center for Christian gatherings. In Jerusalem this was dangerous because Christians had had to give up worship in temple and synagogues due of the threat of persecution.[2]

It is interesting to note that in the Greek and Roman culture, women participated in festive meals. Hence it is more likely that women would participate in the "breaking of the bread" in the Hellenistic Christian house churches than in the Hebrew Christian communities.[3]

Mary was probably a widow. She was the mother of John Mark, a coworker of Paul and an aunt or cousin of Barnabas, a missionary apostle in the church at Jerusalem. Mary knew

Peter. Since her son worked with Paul, she probably had some connection with Paul.

The Acts of the Apostles tells the story of Peter's amazing escape from prison to Mary's home. On the night Peter was to be judged, an angel appeared, a light shone in the cell, and his chains fell off. The angel instructed Peter to follow him. He obeyed the angel's orders but thought he was seeing a vision. Then, suddenly, Peter realized that the angel was sent by God to deliver him from the violent persecution of Herod. As soon as he understood this, Peter immediately went to Mary's house church where many members of the Christian community were praying. Peter knocked at the gate. Rhoda, the maid, came to answer and upon recognizing Peter's voice, she was so overwhelmed that, instead of letting Peter in, she rushed back to tell the community—leaving Peter standing at the gate. At first, the community didn't believe her. Meanwhile Peter kept knocking, and when they opened the gate, they were overjoyed to see him. Peter then told them the details of his miraculous rescue. He instructed them to tell James and the other believers. Then he left (see Acts 12:6–17).

The brief passage that mentions Mary's name and describes her house church is significant for two reasons. First, the very mention of her name reflects her prominence in the community. Second, it is revealing that Peter, after his release from prison, goes immediately to her home. It seems that Mary's house church was the place where believers in Jerusalem came regularly to pray and to seek refuge when their lives were threatened. According to the scriptures, there were a number of other women whose names and house churches were also mentioned. Like Mary, their homes also were the first Christian "churches." These include: Chloe (1 Cor 1:11); Lydia (Acts 16:40); Nympha (Col 4:15) and Prisca (Rom 16:3,5).[4]

The text makes it evident that women and men in the early Christian movement formed a praying community. No longer was there a woman's court and the court of Israel, "where many had gathered and were praying" (Acts 12:12). This was a major break with custom, which reflected the influence of Jesus. Janice Nunnally-Cox observes: "The house of Mary and the other women's houses are revolutionary; they house dissidents, they break custom, they initiate new worship, they continue the teachings of Jesus."[5]

As a champion of dissident Christians and a leader who presided at Eucharist, Mary is one who understands our quest to initiate new paradigms of worship, prayer, and Christian community today. From all over the globe, sisters, daughters, mothers, grandmothers, women of many cultures are sharing their visions and their dreams to birth a new voice for prayer and worship. Women's prayer groups have appeared in many places and are exploring a rich variety of resources and styles. As the bondage of racism, sexism, militarism, materialism, and ageism continues, the proclamation of the Word, the beauty of praise, the joy of song and dance, the power of ritual are needed all the more to open our hearts to justice, peace, and equality. Mary is a companion whom we can invite to join us on our journey to inclusive, liberating, vibrant communal worship.

REFLECTION

"As soon as he realized this, he [Peter] went to the house of Mary, the mother of John whose other name was Mark, where many had gathered and were praying. When he knocked at the outer gate, a maid named Rhoda came to answer. On recognizing Peter's voice, she was so overjoyed that, instead of opening the gate, she ran in and announced that Peter was standing at the gate. They said to her, 'You are out of your mind!' But she insisted that it was so. They said, 'It is his angel.' Meanwhile Peter continued knocking; and when they opened the gate, they saw him and were amazed. He motioned to them with his hand to be silent, and described for them how God had brought him out of the prison. And he added, 'Tell this to James and to the believers.' Then he left and went to another place" (Acts 12:12–17).

DISCUSSION STARTERS

1. What is the significance of Mary presiding at Eucharist in her house church in Jerusalem? Do you suppose John Mark, Peter, or Barnabas were ever present at these eucharistic celebrations? If so, how do you think they responded?

2. Are women today leaders in communities similar to house churches? Do they preside at Eucharist in these communities? What impact do women who preside at Eucharist in the Anglican and Lutheran traditions have on the people of God today? Should women, in your opinion, preside at Eucharist in the Roman Catholic tradition? in the Orthodox tradition?

3. Why is it important to be a member of a praying community?

4. What new forms or expressions of prayer, ritual, and liturgy are women's communities experimenting with today? What new forms or expressions of prayer, ritual, and liturgy are renewal movements in the Church experimenting with today? What impact do these new expressions or experiences have on you? the local community? the universal Church?

PRAYER EXPERIENCE

1. Imagine God as a sister-companion accompanying you through life…. Begin this prayer experience by inhaling Sister-God's tremendous love for life…. Exhale any negative thoughts and feelings…. Recall that Sister-God is always with you…with all people…with all creation…. You have something special you want to share with her…. Sister-God wants to give you a gift….

2. Imagine you are Mary in the house church in Jerusalem…. It is such a hectic place…. People are coming and going…. Herod's persecution has caused trouble for the community…. Peter is in prison…. The community is gathering today for Eucharist…. The singing starts…prayers of praise and thanksgiving fill the room…. You break the bread and pour the wine…. Everyone shares in the bread and wine…. The community shares their gifts and blessings…. As the celebration concludes, Rhoda comes in…. She says that Peter is at the gate…. The group laughs… tells her that she is crazy…. Then a few members go to the gate to check it out…. Sure enough, here comes Peter…. He tells the story of the angel and his release…. Everyone is amazed…. Before he departs, Peter tells the community to share the good news with James and the believers…. Now you want to share some thoughts…feelings…insights with the members of your house church before they leave….

3. Pretend that you belong to a faith community where women preside at Eucharist…. Be attentive to Christ's nurturing presence…. Abundant grace surrounds you….

4. Name ways that women image Sister-God in the contemporary world.

   Offer thanks for woman presence in your life.

5. Compose a prayer, psalm, song, dance, or design an art piece expressing your gratitude for your relationships... with Sister-God...with significant women in your life....

6. Compose an original eucharistic prayer and share it with others in a praying community....

7. Be aware of how you can become "bread broken" by sharing, caring, and serving others in your city....

THECLA

⟨꙳⟩

The *Acts of Paul and Thecla* is one of the rare, second-century texts of early Christianity from Asia Minor wherein a woman occupies the central role. Some scholars believe it has a historical basis. Others think that originally it was an oral folk tale told by women storytellers that later was written down in a form that resembles the Hellenistic romance.[1] This popular, apocryphal book was translated from the original Greek into Latin, Syrian, Armenian, Slavonic, and Arabic. It tells the exciting story of Thecla's conversion by Saint Paul and recounts her courage throughout her various trials.[2]

Thecla convinces Paul to accept her as a missionary disciple and coworker. After Paul takes her with him to Antioch, a man named Alexander falls in love with her. When this occurs, Paul denies knowing Thecla and abandons her. Then, Alexander, assuming that he can have his way with her, attempts to rape her, but Thecla prevails. Later, Alexander accuses Thecla before the governor, and she is condemned to fight the wild beasts. When Alexander brings Thecla to the arena, a wealthy woman friend, Tryphaena, intercedes for divine protection for Thecla, and Alexander runs away in fear. Then the governor orders soldiers to take her to the arena, but the women maintain control, and Tryphaena leads Thecla to the games. There Thecla is stripped and thrown into the arena with the wild beasts. The men in the crowd condemn Thecla, but the women condemn the city for its lawlessness. "But the women with their children cried out from above saying: 'O God, an impious judgment is come to pass in this city!' The women said: 'May the city perish for this lawlessness!'"³

According to the story, a powerful lioness defends Thecla against a lion and a bear sent to devour her. The lioness dies trying to rescue Thecla. Then the women in the crowd take a courageous stance on her behalf. They throw perfumes and flowers and overwhelm the new beasts sent by the men. Finally, Tryphaena passes out in the arena. When this happens, Alexander fears retribution because Tryphaena is a relative of Caesar. At this time the governor summons Thecla and asks her to explain why the beasts have not killed her. She takes this opportunity to give him a mini-lesson in the Christian faith. The governor releases Thecla and "all the women" praise God, "who has delivered Thecla."⁴

In her commentary on the text, Sheila E. McGinn observes that the Greco-Roman society of the day assumed that every woman must belong to a man:

> [I]n the storyteller's view, the rejection of Roman authority and a woman's refusal of sexual activity are functionally equivalent and need not be distinguished…. God protects and delivers a woman who opposes the sex-role definitions of the city, showing God's power over the culture as a whole. Female chastity and divine power are victorious over male law and aggression.⁵

The male/female tension is further explored when the lioness fights the bear and lion sent to kill Thecla. This demonstrates that female solidarity with Thecla and her message includes earth's female creatures. Thecla's faith overcomes any rift between women and the female animals (symbolized by the lioness). The lioness dies as a martyr fighting to save the human martyr, Thecla. The grief that the women (in the crowd) display for the lioness expresses this powerful solidarity.[6]

In addition to showing great courage and experiencing many miracles, Thecla baptizes herself. Many beasts were ready to attack Thecla "while she stood and stretched out her hands and prayed." When she had finished her prayer, she turned and saw a great pit full of water, and said: "Now is the time for me to wash." And she threw herself in, saying: "In the name of Jesus Christ I baptize myself on the last day!"[7] The *Acts of Thecla* were a protest against the practice that only males could baptize, with the exception of women deaconesses who assisted at baptisms in the East.[8]

Although there were restrictions on women teaching the Christian message at this time (cf. 1 Tm 2:11–12), Thecla breaks through this barrier and instructs converts at the request of Saint Paul.

> So Thecla went in with her and rested in her house for eight days, instructing her in the word of God, so that the majority of the maidservants also believed, and there was great joy in the house…. And Thecla arose and said to Paul: "I am going to Iconium." But Paul said: "Go and teach the word of God!"…After enlightening many with the word of God she slept with a noble sleep.[9]

The baptizing and teaching of Thecla became a model for Christian women, a fact attested to by the intense opposition of second-century writer Tertullian:

> But the impudence of the woman who assumed the right to teach is evidently not going to abrogate to her the right to baptize as well…certain acts of Paul, which are falsely so named, claim the example of Thecla for allowing women to teach and to baptize…. How could

we believe that Paul should give a female power to teach and to baptize, when he did not allow a woman even to learn by her own right?[10]

There is a major difference between the presentation of women and men in the *Acts of Thecla* and that given in the *Acts of Paul*.

The redactor who included Thecla's story in the *Acts of Paul* emphasized the importance of men, and especially of Paul. Women are subordinate to Paul; when they are important in the text, they either oppose Paul or are the channel for male resistance to him. In sum, according to the *Acts of Paul*, women are a threat to the Christian mission. In the *Acts of Thecla*, on the other hand, while portraying women and men as both involved in Christianity, it is women who are the more faithful advocates. In this text, Paul is depicted in a negative way. He betrays Thecla and leaves her to be devoured by wild beasts. At first, Paul even opposes Thecla's baptism and teaching ministry. Yet God affirms her call through signs and miracles. Only then does Paul support Thecla's ministry. The *Acts of Thecla* reveals the courage of a woman "apostle" who commits herself totally to proclaiming the gospel. Her fidelity to Christ is her strength in her great sufferings, including the threat of martyrdom. [11]

By presenting a woman apostle, the *Acts of Thecla* stirs hope in women who are called to preach, teach, and live the fullness of their baptism today. This story reminds us to live in harmony with all earth's creatures. The story of Thecla also reveals the overwhelming power of women's solidarity— women supporting other women—to liberate, heal, and transform our world. In the end, no threat, harassment, attack can limit the possibilities or places that our dreams and divine love can take us together. "For I am convinced that neither death, nor life, nor angels, nor rulers, nor things present, nor things to come, nor powers, nor height, nor depth, nor anything else in all creation, will be able to separate us from the love of God in Christ Jesus..." (Rom 8:38).

REFLECTION

"But the women were panic-stricken, and cried out before the judgment-seat: An evil judgment!... But the women with their children cried out from above, saying: 'O God, an impious judgment is come to pass in this city!'...The women said: 'May the city perish for this lawlessness! Slay us all, Proconsul! A bitter sight, an evil judgment!'... And the crowd of the women raised a great shout.... And the women mourned the more, since the lioness which helped her was dead.... But as other more terrible beasts were let loose, the women cried aloud, and some threw petals, others nard, others cassia, others amomum, so that there was an abundance of perfumes. And all the beasts let loose were overpowered as if by sleep, and did not touch her.... But all the women cried out with a loud voice, and, as with one mouth, gave praise to God, saying: 'One is God, who has delivered Thecla!' so that all the city was shaken by the sound."[12]

DISCUSSION STARTERS

1. "The men in the crowd condemned Thecla but the women condemned the city for its lawlessness." According to the *Acts of Paul*, women were a threat to the Christian mission. The *Acts of Thecla*, on the other hand, portrays women as its more faithful advocates. What impact have these two different mind-sets had on attitudes toward

women in the past? Have these attitudes changed in our times? Why? Why not?

2. Why is it important for women, and men, to live in harmony with earth's creatures?

3. How can women expressing solidarity with other women make a difference in our society?

4. What threats, harassments, attacks do women experience today in living the Christian message?

Prayer Experience

1. Breathe slowly and deeply several times. Become aware of each breath as you inhale and exhale. Imagine each breath you take as filled with the infinite love of God for you…for all people…for all creation….

2. Read the reflection from Thecla slowly and thoughtfully.

3. Imagine that you are Thecla, naked, in the arena with the beasts…. The lioness is attacking the lion and the bear sent to devour you…. You look on in horror as she is torn to pieces…. Your friend Tryphaena faints…. Alexander, your accuser, flees…. The men in the crowd shout horrible words of condemnation…. The women in the crowd rise to your defense…. They throw flowers and perfume at the beasts…. Suddenly, the animals calm down and do not attempt to attack you…. Everyone in the crowd is shocked…. You are brought before the governor…. Now you are clothed…. He asks you to explain why the beasts have not killed you…. You share with him your love for Christ and your devotion to the gospel…. Then he releases you, and all the women praise God for your deliverance…. Now you join Tryphaena and your women supporters in a celebration…. You begin by expressing your gratitude to these women…. Then you go on to share your

innermost feelings about this powerful experience.... The women give you a symbol of their love and support for you.... You delight in their strength....

4. Reflect on women, like Thecla, who have the courage to fight sexual harassment, threats, discrimination in their lives....

5. Be aware of the hundreds of thousands of women who have suffered physical, emotional, and sexual abuse...torture...rape...and death...and/or who have lost spouses, children, family members because of human and civil rights violations in this century.... Mourn with them for their sufferings, losses, and pain....

6. Create a litany, prayer, poem, or a symbol to express your support for these courageous women.... And/or anoint one another with the oil of integrity, courage, and healing....

7. Take a walk.... Breathe deeply.... Look up at the sky.... Smile.... Hug a tree.... Pet an animal.... Contemplate earth's creatures.... Celebrate your connectedness with creation in whatever way(s) feels most comfortable and fun for you....

NOTES

Sarah

1. Trevor Dennis, *Sarah Laughed*, Nashville, TN: Abingdon Press, 1994, p. 44.
2. Sharon Pace Jeansonne, *The Women of Genesis*, Minneapolis, MN: Fortress Press, 1990, p. 28.
3. Savina Teubal, "Sarah and Hagar: Matriarchs and Visionaries" in *A Feminist Companion to Genesis*, ed. by Athalya Brenner, Sheffield, England: Sheffield Academic Press, 1993, p. 236.
4. Elsa Tamez, "The Woman Who Complicated the History of Salvation" in *New Eyes for Reading*, ed. by John S. Pobee and Barbel Von Wartenberg-Potter, Oak Park, IL: Meyer Stone Books, 1986, p. 12.
5. Janice Nunnally-Cox, *ForeMothers*, New York, NY: Seabury Press, 1981, p. 9.
6. Miriam Therese Winter, *WomanWisdom*, New York, NY: Crossroad, 1991, p. 17.

Hagar

1. Elsa Tamez, "The Woman Who Complicated the History of Salvation" in *New Eyes for Reading*, ed. by John S. Pobee and Barbel Von Wartenberg-Potter, Oak Park, IL: Meyer Stone Books, 1986, p. 13.
2. Ibid., p. 13.
3. Miriam Therese Winter, *WomanWisdom*, New York, NY: Crossroad, 1991, p. 38.
4. Savina Teubal, *Hagar, the Egyptian: The Lost Tradition of the Matriarchs*, San Francisco: HarperCollins, 1990, pp. 127, 200.
5. Alice Ogden Bellis, *Helpmates, Harlots, and Heroes*, Louisville, KY: Westminster/John Knox, 1994, pp. 78–79.

6. Phyllis Trible, *Texts of Terror*, London: SCM Press, Ltd., 1984, p. 28.

Miriam

1. Mary Zimmer, *Sister Images*, Nashville, TN: Abingdon Press, 1993, pp. 21–22.
2. Renita J. Weems, *Just a Sister Away*, San Diego, CA: Lura Media, 1998, p. 73.
3. Rita J. Burns, *Has the Lord Indeed Spoken Only through Moses? A Study of the Biblical Portrait of Miriam*, SBL Dissertation Series 84, Atlanta, GA: Scholars Press, 1987, p. 124.
4. Katharine Doob Sakenfeld, "Numbers," in *The Women's Bible Commentary*, edited by Carol A. Newsom and Sharon H. Ringe, Louisville, KY: Westminster/John Knox Press, 1992, p. 48.
5. Phyllis Trible, "Bringing Miriam Out of the Shadows," *Bible Review* (February 1989), p. 21.
6. Ibid., p. 25.
7. Miriam Therese Winter, *WomanWisdom*, New York, NY: Crossroad, 1991, pp. 77–78.

Deborah

1. Miriam Therese Winter, *WomanWitness*, New York, NY: Crossroad, 1992, p. 36.
2. Mieke Bal, *Death and Disymmetry: The Politics of Coherence in the Book of Judges*, Chicago, IL: University of Chicago Press, 1988, p. 209.
3. Julia Esquivel, "Liberation Theology and Women" in *New Eyes for Reading: Biblical and Theological Reflections by Women from the Third World*, edited by John S. Pobee and Barbel von Wartenberg-Potter, Oak Park, IL: Meyer Stone Books, 1986, p. 22.
4. Lillian Sigal, "Models of Love and Hate," *Daughters of Sarah* 16, no. 2 (March/April 1990), pp. 8, 10.
5. Gale A. Yee, "By the Hand of a Woman: The Metaphor of the Woman Warrior in Judges 4," in *Women, War, and Metaphor: Language and Society in the Study of the Hebrew Bible*, edited by Claudia V. Camp and Carole R. Fontaine, *Semeia* 61 (1993), p. 100, 112–114; cited in Alice Ogden Bellis, *Helpmates, Harlots, and Heroes*, Louisville, KY: Westminster/John Knox Press, 1994, p. 118.
6. William E. Phipps, *Assertive Women*, Westport, CT and London: Greenwood Press, 1992, pp. 43–44.

7. Elizabeth Cady Stanton, ed., *The Woman's Bible*, New York, NY: European Publishing Company, 1895, 2:21.

8. Norma Rosen, *Biblical Women Unbound*, Philadelphia, PA, and Jerusalem: The Jewish Publication Society, 1996, p. 140.

9. Denise Lardner Carmody, *Biblical Women: Contemporary Reflections on Scriptural Texts*, New York, NY: Crossroad, 1988, p. 29.

Ruth

1. Patricia Karlin-Neuman, "The Journey Toward Life" in *Reading Ruth: Contemporary Women Reclaim a Sacred Story*, edited by Judith A. Kates and Gail Twensky Reimer, New York, NY: Ballantine, 1994, p. 127.

2. Mary Zimmer, *Sister Images*, Nashville, TN: Abingdon, 1993, p. 128.

3. Donna Nolan Fewell and David Miller Gunn, *Compromising Redemption: Relating Characters in the Book of Ruth: Literary Currents in Biblical Interpretation*, Louisville, KY: Westminster/John Knox, 1990, p. 105.

4. Renita Weems, *Just a Sister Away: A Womanist Vision of Women's Relationships in the Bible*, San Diego, CA: Lura Media, 1989, p. 33, 31.

5. Andre La Cocque, *The Feminist Unconventional: Four Subversive Figures in Israel's Tradition*, Minneapolis, MN: Fortress Press, 1990, pp. 86–87.

6. Ibid., p. 105.

7. Claudia Camp, *Wisdom and the Feminine in the Book of Proverbs*, Decatur, GA: Almond Press, 1985, p. 128, 129.

8. Mieke Bal, *Lethal Love: Feminist Literary Readings of Biblical Love Stories*, Indiana: Indiana University, 1987, p. 71.

9. Murray D. Gow, *The Book of Ruth: Its Structure, Theme and Purpose*, London, England: Apollos 1992, p. 135.

Esther

1. Edith Deen, *All of the Women of the Bible*, San Francisco, CA: HarperCollins, 1983, pp. 146–147.

2. Ibid., pp. 147–151.

3. Sidnie Ann White, "Esther" in *The Women's Bible Commentary*, edited by Carol A. Newsom and Sharon H. Ringe, Louisville, KY: Westminster/John Knox Press, 1992, p. 126.

4. Renita Weems, *Just a Sister Away: A Womanist Vision of Women's Relationships in the Bible*, San Diego, CA: Lura Media, 1988, p. 103, 105.
5. Ibid., p. 108.
6. Mary Gendler, "The Restoration of Vashti" in *The Jewish Woman: New Perspectives*, edited by Elizabeth Koltun, New York, NY: Schocken, 1976, p. 247.
7. Marjory Zoet Bankson, *Braided Streams: Esther and a Woman's Way of Growing*, San Diego, CA: Lura Media, 1985, p. 111.
8. Ibid., p. 115.

Judith

1. Miriam Therese Winter, *WomanWitness*, New York, NY: Crossroad, 1992, p. 111.
2. Toni Craven, "Tradition and Convention in the Book of Judith" in *The Bible and Feminist Hermeneutics*, edited by Mary Ann Tolbert, Semeia 28 (1983), p. 52.
3. Patricia Montley, "Judith in the Fine Arts: The Appeal of the Archetypal Androgyne," *Anima* 4 (1978) 40, cited in Andre La Cocque, *The Feminist Unconventional: Four Subversive Figures in Israel's Tradition*, Minneapolis, MN: Fortress Press, 1990, p. 38.
4. La Cocque, *The Feminist Unconventional*, p. 48.
5. Ibid., p. 39.
6. Alice Ogden Bellis, *Helpmates, Harlots, Heroes*, Louisville, KY: Westminster/John Knox Press, 1994, p. 222.
7. Miriam Therese Winter, *WomanWitness*, pp. 117–120.

The Samaritan Woman

1. Mary Zimmer, *Sister Images*, Nashville, TN: Abingdon Press, 1993, p. 44.
2. Rose Sallberg Kam, *Their Stories, Our Stories*, New York, NY: Continuum, 1995, pp. 213–214.
3. Rachel Conrad Wahlberg, *Jesus According to a Woman*, Mahwah, NJ: Paulist Press, 1986, p. 90.
4. Rose Sallberg Kam, *Their Stories, Our Stories*, pp. 215–216.

Martha

1. Rose Sallberg Kam, *Their Stories, Our Stories*, New York, NY: Continuum, 1995, p. 219.

2. Mary Zimmer, *Sister Images*, Nashville, TN: Abingdon Press, 1993, p. 78.
3. Elisabeth Schussler Fiorenza, *In Memory of Her*, New York, NY: Crossroad, 1986, p. 165.
4. Rose Sallberg Kam, op cit., p. 220.

Woman with the Flow of Blood

1. Elisabeth Schussler Fiorenza, "The Quest for the Johannine School: The Apocalypse and the Fourth Gospel," *NTS* 23 (1976/77) 402–407 cited in *In Memory of Her*, p. 124.
2. Marie-Eloise Rosenblatt, *Where Can We Find Her?* Mahwah, NJ: Paulist Press, 1991. pp. 32–33.
3. Rose Sallberg Kam, *Their Stories, Our Stories*, New York, NY: Continuum Publishing Company, 1995, p. 189.

The Canaanite Woman

1. Mary Zimmer, *Sister Images*, Nashville, TN: Abingdon Press, 1993, p. 140.
2. Ibid., pp. 140–141.
3. Elisabeth Schussler Fiorenza, *In Memory of Her*, New York, NY: Crossroad, 1986, p. 137.
4. Leonard Swidler, *Biblical Affirmations of Woman*, Philadelphia, PA: Westminster Press, 1979, p. 182.

Mary of Magdala

1. Mary Zimmer, *Sister Images*, Nashville, TN: Abingdon Press, 1993, p. 82.
2. Ibid., p. 82.
3. The Inclusive New Testament, Brentwood, Maryland: Priests For Equality, p. 204.
4. Janice Nunnally-Cox, *ForeMothers*, New York, NY: Seabury Press, 1981, p. 115.
5. Edgar Hennecke, *New Testament Apocrypha*, ed. W. Schneemelcher, trans. R. McL. Wilson, Philadelphia, PA: Westminster Press, 1965, 2.379f. cited in Elisabeth Schussler Fiorenza, *In Memory of Her*, New York: Crossroad, 1986, p. 305.
6. Elisabeth Schussler Fiorenza, *In Memory of Her*, p. 306.
7. Raymond E. Brown, "Roles of Women in the Fourth Gospel," p. 692 cited in Leonard Swidler, *Biblical Affirmations of Woman*, p. 223.

8. Bernard of Clairvaux Migne, *Patrologia Latina*, Vol. 183, col. 1148 cited in Swidler, *Biblical Affirmations of Woman*, p. 209.

9. *The Inclusive New Testament*, Brentwood, Maryland: Priests For Equality, p. 204.

10. Elaine Pagels, *The Gnostic Gospels*, New York, NY: Random House, 1979, p. xv.

11. Berlin Gnostic Codex 8502 7.18 cited in Fiorenza, *In Memory of Her*, p. 306.

Woman Who Anoints Jesus' Head

1. Janice Nunnally-Cox, *ForeMothers*, New York, NY: Seabury Press, 1981, p. 104.

2. Cf. J. K. Elliott, "The Anointing of Jesus," Exp. Time. 85 (1974) 105–7 cited in Elisabeth Schussler Fiorenza, *In Memory of Her*, New York, NY: Crossroad, 1986, p. xiv.

3. Ross Saunders, *Outrageous Women, Outrageous God*, Alexandria, Australia: E. J. Dwyer Ltd., 1996, p. 53.

4. Mary Zimmer, *Sister Images*, Nashville, TN: Abingdon Press, 1993, p. 39.

5. L. W. Countryman, "Christian Equality and the Early Catholic Episcopate," *Anglican Theological Review* 63 (1981) 115–38:115. cited in Fiorenza, In Memory of Her, p. xiv.

Mary, Mother of Jesus

1. Lawrence S. Cunningham, *The Catholic Experience*, New York, NY: Crossroad, 1985, pp. 168–169.

2. Ann E. Carr, *Transforming Grace: Christian Tradition and Women's Experience*, San Francisco, CA: HarperCollins, 1988, p. 193.

3. Leonard Swidler, *Biblical Affirmations of Woman*, Philadelphia, PA: Westminster Press, 1979, p. 266.

Junia

1. *The Homilies of St. John Chrysostom*, Nicene and Post-Nicene Fathers, Series 1, 11:555 Wm B. Eerdmans Publishing Co., 1956 cited in Swidler, *Biblical Affirmations of Woman*, p. 299.

2. Leonard Swidler, *Biblical Affirmations of Woman*, p. 299.

3. Bernadette J. Brooten, "Junia…Outstanding Among the Apostles (Rom 16:7)" in *Woman Priests*, ed. Leonard S. Swidler and Arlene Swidler, New York, NY: Paulist Press, 1977, pp. 141–44; cited in

Elizabeth Castelli, "Romans" in *Searching the Scriptures*, vol. 2 edited by Elisabeth Schussler Fiorenza, New York, NY: Crossroad, 1994, pp. 279–280.

4. Ross Saunders, *Outrageous Women, Outrageous God*, Alexandria, Australia: E. J. Dwyer, 1996, p. 117.

5. H. A. Guy, *New Testament Prophecy: Its Origins and Significance*, London: Epworth Press, 1947, pp. 119–142; cited in Elisabeth Schussler Fiorenza, *In Memory of Her*, pp. 172–173.

6. *In Memory of Her*, p. 172.

Phoebe

1. Reta Halteman Finger, "Phoebe, Role Model for Leaders," *Daughters of Sarah* (XIV:5, March–April 1988), pp. 5–7.

2. Elisabeth Schussler Fiorenza, *In Memory of Her*, p. 180.

3. Ibid., p. 48.

4. Carolyn D. Baker, "Phoebe, Radiant One," *Paraclete* 29:2 (Spring 1995), 13–14.

Prisca (Priscilla)

1. Miriam Therese Winter, *WomanWord*, New York, NY: Crossroad, 1990, p. 233.

2. Elisabeth Schussler Fiorenza, "The Quest for the Johannine School: The Apocalypse and the Fourth Gospel," NTS 23, (1976/77) 402–427 cited in Fiorenza, *In Memory of Her*, p. 179.

3. Roger Gryson; trans. Jean Laporte and Mary Louise Hall, *The Ministry of Women in the Early Church*, Collegeville, Minnesota: Liturgical Press, 1980, pp. 4–5.

4. Edith Deen, *All of the Women of the Bible*, pp. 228–229

5. Ibid. p. 229.

6. Elisabeth Schussler Fiorenza, *In Memory of Her*, p. 179.

Lydia

1. Edith Deen, *All of the Women of the Bible*, San Francisco, CA: Harper and Row, 1955, pp. 222–224.

2. Elisabeth Schussler Fiorenza, *In Memory of Her*, p. 180.

3. Rev. W. Derek Thomas, "The Place of Women in the Church at Philippi" in *The Expository Times* 83: Jan. 1972, p. 118.

4. Dorothy Irvin, "Archaeology Supports Women's Ordination," in *The Witness* (vol. 63, no. 2, February 1980), p. 6. cited in Janice

Nunnally-Cox, *ForeMothers*, New York: Seabury Press, 1981, pp. 128–129.
5. Mary Lou Sleevi, *Women of the Word*, Notre Dame, Indiana: Ave Maria Press, 1989, p. 96.

Mary, Mother of John Mark

1. Miriam Therese Winter, *WomanWord*, p. 196.
2. Ross Saunders, *Outrageous Women, Outrageous God*, Alexandria, Australia: E. J. Dwyer Ltd, 1996, pp. 102–103.
3. J. D. Quinn, "Ordination in the Pastoral Epistles," *Communio* 8 (1981) 358–369, cited in Elisabeth Schussler Fiorenza, *In Memory of Her*, p. 166.
4. Janice Nunnally-Cox, *ForeMothers*, New York: Seabury, 1981, p. 125.
5. Ibid., pp. 125–126.

Thecla

1. Willy Rordorf, "Tradition and Composition in the Acts of Thecla: The State of the Question," *Semeia* 38, 1986, p. 44.
2. *The Acts of Paul and Thecla, New Testament Apocrypha*, Vol. 2, pp. 360–363, cited in Leonard Swidler, *Biblical Affirmations of Woman*, pp. 318–319.
3. Ibid., p. 319.
4. Sheila E. McGinn, *The Acts of Thecla*, in *Searching the Scriptures*, edited by Elisabeth Schussler Fiorenza, New York; Crossroad, 1994, pp. 817–818.
5. Ibid., pp. 816, 818.
6. Ibid., pp. 817–818.
7. *The Acts of Paul and Thecla, New Testament Apocrypha*, Vol. 2, p. 362 cited in Leonard Swidler, *Biblical Affirmations of Woman*, p. 319.
8. Leonard Swidler, *Biblical Affirmations of Woman*, p. 319.
9. *The Acts of Paul and Thecla, New Testament Apocrypha*, Vol. 2, pp. 363–364, cited in Leonard Swidler, *Biblical Affirmations of Woman*, pp. 319–320.
10. Tertullian, *De Baptismo* 17.4 cited in Leonard Swidler, *Biblical Affirmations of Woman*, p. 320.
11. Sheila E. McGinn, *The Acts of Thecla*, in *Searching the Scriptures*, edited by Elisabeth Schussler Fiorenza, New York: Crossroad, 1994, pp. 819–820.

12. *The Acts of Paul and Thecla, New Testament Apocrypha*, Vol. 2, pp. 360–363, cited in Leonard Swidler, *Biblical Affirmations of Woman*, p. 319.

Recommended Reading
on Biblical Women

Bellis, Alice Ogden. *Helpmates, Harlots, Heroes*, Louisville, Kentucky: Westminster/John Knox 1994.

This comprehensive book shares the work of feminist biblical scholars who have examined women's stories in the last twenty-five years. These stories are moving accounts of women in the Hebrew scriptures—stories that have profoundly influenced how women understand themselves. The book contains scholarly notes and bibliography.

Fiorenza, Elizabeth Schussler. *In Memory of Her*. New York: Crossroad, 1983.

This scholarly treatise brings to consciousness women who played an important role in the origins of Christianity. It represents a shift from an androcentric to a feminist interpretation and a reconstruction of women's early Christian history. A groundbreaking book, and a first within the discipline of New Testament studies, it is must-reading for students of the early Church and New Testament, as well as for feminists.

Nunnally-Cox, Janice. *ForeMothers*, New York: Seabury, 1981.

A clear and popular presentation of the women of the Hebrew and Christian scriptures that discusses the story of Sara and Hagar, Leah and Rachel, Dinah, Miriam, Deborah and Jael, Hannah, Michal and Abigail, the woman with a hemorrhage, the Syrophoenician woman, the adulterous woman, Tabitha, Euodia and Syntyche, among others. This is a helpful resource for all persons interested in women in the Bible and an inspira-tion for contemporary women and men in their search for God.

Saunders, Ross. *Outrageous Women, Outrageous God*, Alex-andria, Australia: E. J. Dwyer, 1996.

This innovative approach presents the countercultural stand of Jesus and Paul toward women. The author uses the word "out-rageous" to describe how far women in the early Christian com-munity journeyed beyond acceptable norms. "That God would at times encourage such behavior means that to some extent," comments Saunders, "God is the origin of this outrageousness." A clearly written, wonderful resource for Bible study groups.

Sleevi, Mary Lou. *Sisters and Prophets*, Notre Dame, Indiana: Ave Maria Press, 1993.

Mary Lou Sleevi's sacred art and stories portray twelve women of faith. Through their visionary lives and prophetic voices, we learn new things about ourselves and God. Like her previous bestseller, *Women of the Word* (Ave Maria Press, 1989), this beauti-ful book invites us to contemplate the strength and courage of our spiritual foremothers.

Swidler, Leonard. *Biblical Affirmations of Woman*, Philadel-phia: Westminster Press, 1979.

This is a scholarly treatise on what the Bible says about women. It contains Jewish rabbinic sources and the writings of the early Church. It is an excellent reference book, an ideal resource for individual or group study.

Winter, Miriam Therese. *WomanWord*, New York: Crossroad, 1990.

This feminist lectionary provides creative celebrations that include biographical information, shared discussion questions, and original psalms on New Testament women such as Anna, the woman who anoints Jesus' head, the poor widow, the woman at the well, Martha and Mary, Mary Magdalene, Jairus' daughter, Rhoda, Lydia, Phoebe, Prisca, Peter's mother-in-law, Lois and Eunice, and many others.

Winter, Miriam Therese. *WomanWisdom*, Part One, New York: Crossroad, 1991.

In this book liturgist Winter presents fifty provocative celebrations for women of the Hebrew scriptures—both "women whose stories have been told," like Eve and Sarah and Rebekah, and women whose stories must be told, such as Cozi and Zipporah and Keturah. A powerful book for women—and men—of all denominations who want to celebrate our foremothers and foresisters in the faith.

Winter, Miriam Therese. *WomanWitness*, Part Two, New York: Crossroad, 1992.

In this last of her three companion volumes Winter presents fifty more services for women of the Hebrew scriptures. There are innovative liturgies for women like Tamar, Poiphar's wife, Pharaoh's daughter, Deborah, Delilah, Ruth, Naomi, Bathsheba, Jezebel, and the women often forgotten: the prostitutes, midwives, maids, servants, and slaves.

Zimmer, Mary. *Sister Images*, Nashville: Abingdon Press, 1993.

A collection of twenty commentaries and guided imagery meditations written especially to help contemporary women make connections between their own lives and those of their female biblical sisters. It is ideal for personal devotion, spiritual formation, and study groups. This book bridges the gap between biblical interpretation, feminist theology, and women in the Church.

ACKNOWLEDGMENTS

In writing this book, I am especially grateful to my family and friends. Their gift of faith and friendship has touched me deeply.

I am especially thankful to my parents, Bridie and Jack Meehan, who taught me so much about God's love by their love for me. I am also grateful to my aunt, Molly McCarthy, who reflected an adventurous love for life and is now with God in eternal joy; my brothers and sisters-in-law, Sean and Nancy, Patrick and Valerie, whose courage and strength are a constant source of inspiration to me. I thank my niece and nephew, Katie and Danny, for teaching me how to play and delight in the wonders of God in the precious present moments of life.

I am also grateful to the following male friends and colleagues who have been supportive in my journey: Joe Mulqueen, John Weyand, Francis L. Keefe, Charlie Davis, Phil Thomas, Jim Webster, John Adams, Jay McDonald, Ray McGovern, Terry Danner, Fritz Warren, Bob Bowen, Walter Montondon, Ray Buchanan, Mike Marshall, Larry Skummer, Bennie Rossler, Dick Guertin, John Mattias, Bill Dillon, Connie Coakley, Douglas Sandiego, Kevin Voelker, Rafael Sandiego.

I owe a special debt of gratitude to Marcia Tibbitts, Regina Madonna Oliver, and Patricia A. Kossmann who edited and prepared this manuscript for publication.

ABOUT THE AUTHOR

Bridget Mary Meehan, a Sister for Christian Community (SFCC), holds a master's degree in spirituality and religious education from Catholic University and a doctorate in ministry from Virginia Theological Seminary. She is a spiritual director, conference speaker, consultant in women's spirituality, and author of several books, including *Praying With Celtic Holy Women*, *The Healing Power of Prayer*, *Exploring the Feminine Face of God*, *Heart Talks With Mother God*, *Delighting in the Feminine Divine*, and *Affirmations From the Heart of God*.

Dr. Meehan is producer and host of *Godtalk*, a cable television program that aims to nurture the soul, heal the heart, expand consciousness, transform lives, and inspire believers of all faiths.